# ENCOUNTERS

# ENCOUNTERS

## TRAVEL AND MONEY IN THE BYZANTINE WORLD

### EURYDICE GEORGANTELI AND BARRIE COOK

*The* BARBER
Institute of Fine Arts

g

THE
BRITISH
MUSEUM
A Partnership UK project

The Barber Institute of Fine Arts in association with
D Giles Limited, London and The British Museum

© 2006 Barber Institute of Fine Arts

First published in 2006 by GILES

An imprint of D Giles Limited

Kite Studios, Priory Mews,

2B Bassein Park Road,

London, W12 9RY

UK

www.gilesltd.com

ISBN: 1 904832 27 X

For the Barber Institute of Fine Arts:

Eurydice S. Georganteli

For D Giles Limited:

Mercer Design, London, design and layout

David Rose, copy-editor and proof-reader

Produced by D Giles Limited, London

Printed and bound in China

Frontispiece:

**The departure of Nicolò and Matteo Polo from Byzantium (Constantinople)**

Detail of illumination from the *Livre des Merveilles*, c. 1410–12 (author: Marco Polo; manuscript illuminator: maître de la Mazarine)

*Bibliothèque nationale de France, Département des manuscrits occidentaux, MSS Français 2810*

# IN MEMORY OF PHILIP GRIERSON

## Photographic credits

UK: Illustrations for The Henry Barber Coin Collection and The Fitzwilliam Museum by J. Starnes (Oxford Imaging Ltd) & G. Norrie (University of Birmingham).

Illustrations for The British Museum were organised by Janet Larkin, Isabel Assaly and James Rossiter, and the photography was the work of Stephen Dodd (for the Department of Coins and Medals) and Saul Perkins (for the Department of Prehistory and Europe).

Outside the UK: no. 20a: Prof. I. Jordanov, Bulgaria; no. 22: Biblioteca Apostolica Vaticana, Rome; no. 29: Tiroler Landesmuseum Ferdinandeum, Austria; no. 36b: Museum of Tbilisi, Georgia; no. 37: Dr N. Zekos, Greece; nos 46, 47: Bibliothèque nationale, Service de reproduction, France; no. 52: Dr E. Oberländer-Târnoveanu, Romania; nos 16, 55b: RMN, France.

## Acknowledgements

This publication has been made possible by support from AHRC to the Barber Institute of Fine Arts, the Henry Barber Trust, the J.F. Costopoulos Foundation, Spink & Son Ltd and G. Contis. We should also like to thank our colleagues at the Barber Institute of Fine Arts and the Department of Coins and Medals at the Fitzwilliam Museum, C. Entwistle, S. Marzinzik, J. Robinson and D. Thornton in the Department of Prehistory and Europe and all members of the Department of Coins and Medals at the British Museum, Dr E. Oberländer-Târnoveanu at the National Museum of Bucharest and D. Giles, S. McLaughlin and C. Matthews for their kind assistance and advice.

This publication is part of the 21st International Congress of Byzantine Studies

Sponsored by

Arts & Humanities Research Council

# CONTENTS

" There is another mark of the power of the Romans, which God has given them. I mean that it is with their *nomisma* that every nation conducts its commerce, and that it is acceptable in every place from one end of the earth to the other. This *nomisma* is admired by all men and all nations, for in no other nation does such a thing exist. "

Cosmas Indicopleustes, *Christian Topography* (fl. 6th century)

# INTRODUCTION

This quotation from Cosmas Indicopleustes, a Byzantine monk and former merchant, is well known to scholars of Byzantine economic and art history. The nomisma he extols is the Byzantine gold solidus, or bezant as it was known in western sources, a byword for good-quality, stable money from its origin as the solidus of Constantine the Great until well into the 11th century. Its successor, the hyperpyron, was similarly noted in the late 11th century and the 12th. The following chapters are intended to place Cosmas's assertion in context by examining the spread of Byzantine money beyond the borders of the empire, the means through which this occurred and the response of other peoples and cultures to the iconography and value of Byzantine coins.

The role of Byzantine coinage in the medieval east and west was unquestionably widespread and multifaceted: Byzantine coins have been found in burial deposits from Britain to China, were imitated on local coinage across a huge expanse of territory and even used to make purchases at such remote markets as early 13th-century England. Although Cosmas's comment may suggest that Byzantine gold was intended to function as an international coinage and money of account, the private export of actual precious metal outside the Byzantine empire was heavily restricted. Some gold coins would certainly have moved beyond the borders, but most gold exports were undoubtedly related to imperial policies. Impressing foreign rulers, assembling alliances,

ransoming captives and buying off threats, these are just some of the political reasons behind this remarkable movement of coins carried by imperial envoys, soldiers and even princesses and emperors across the medieval world. The coins themselves were important vehicles for cultural encounters, providing a representation of authority to imitate or react against.

The study of Byzantine coins in their archaeological, geographical and historical context offers crucial evidence for the study of medieval economic and cultural encounters. Byzantine coins constantly changed hands in city markets, in rural communities, along routes of pilgrimage, in customs offices at harbours and border points, in transactions between armies and local populations, and as tribute, gifts and dowries between states and their rulers. Byzantine coins found beyond the empire's borders are evidence of the reach of its direct and indirect influence. Byzantine-derived designs used on the coins of other lands similarly echo the transmission of Byzantine culture and ideas of kingship, as Byzantium fluctuated in influence and power through the middle ages. In the same way, the role of foreign coin in Byzantium reflects the impact of other lands on the empire, as armies, church officials and diplomats, merchants, pilgrims and crusaders, allies and enemies, traversed its territory.

London & Birmingham
*Easter 2006*

NORSE

SWEDES

VOLGA BULGARS

*North Sea*

SCOTS

ANGLES

SAXONS

London •

FRISIANS

BRITONS

• Tournai

FRANKS

Metz •

ALANS

• Tours

SLAVS

AVARS

• Chersonesus

*Black Sea*

BURGUNDIANS

Milan •

Ravenna •

Sinope •

Trebizond •

Toulouse •

Marseilles •

LOMBARDS

Dyrrachium •

Serdica •

Constantinople •

Adrianople •

Nicaea •

VISIGOTHS

Rome •

Ohrid •

BENEVENTO

Thessaloniki •

Toledo •

Naples •

Bari •

Ephesos •

Athens •

Antioch •

• Cordoba

Corinth •

Carthage •

Syracuse •

Damascus •

*Mediterranean Sea*

ARABS

Jerusalem •

Alexandria •

# BYZANTIUM AND THE WEST

## I. ALLEGIANCE AND AMBIGUITY: BYZANTIUM AND THE EARLY WESTERN STATES

With the deposition of the last western Roman emperor in 476, the emperor in Constantinople became the only bearer of Roman imperial authority for nearly four centuries. The new kingdoms in the west often accepted, if notionally, the theoretical authority of the eastern emperor, who also asserted his influence in various ways. Diplomats and merchants continued to cross the Mediterranean to North Africa, Italy, France and Spain, and traverse the Roman roads from the Balkans. Following Justinian's reconquest of Italy in the 530s, Rome itself was once again an imperial capital and the residence of the pope, who held influence as both religious leader and Roman official.

The Byzantine empire had a functioning network of diplomatic representatives and agents able to report on developments outside its immediate territory. It is likely that messages and envoys brought notification of the accession of new rulers. Powerful individuals in the west could sometimes feel threatened when they heard of such exchanges by their rivals and enemies. A famous exchange was recorded by the historian Gregory of Tours. An embassy to the east sent by the Frankish king Chilperic I (561–84) eventually returned in 581 bearing spectacularly large gold medallions, each weighing a Roman pound, offered as a gift from Emperor Tiberius Constantine (578–82). Gregory was proudly shown these by the king: 'He showed me the gold coins which the emperor had sent, each of which weigh one pound and had on one side a portrait depicting the emperor'.

The enormous coin-multiples made for 6th- and 7th-century Byzantine emperors were presumably intended to be sent out as gifts on similar occasions and arouse just such a reaction. The ones sent to Chilperic do not survive. A similar large coin-like medallion, equivalent to 36 solidi or half a Roman pound and issued by Justinian I (527–65), was discovered in the 19th century but now survives only in the form of a copy in the British Museum (illus.1). The practice of sending expensive gifts to western rulers may account for the presence in the west of other rich and elaborate objects, including gems and jewelled crosses. Contacts between the Byzantine emperors and Frankish kings continued into the 7th century, as shown by a letter from Heraklios

(610–41) to King Dagobert I (623–39) preserved in a western chronicle. Marriage alliances, however, were not yet part of this interaction between rulers; the only significant proposal of a marriage alliance between an emperor and a western princess occurred in 754, when the growing alliance between the Franks and the pope caused the Byzantines concern.

A different sort of Byzantine gift was the explicit dispatch of coin in bulk. It has been suggested that gold solidi found on islands in the Baltic came from payments to the Ostrogoths, and subsidies to the Franks or Lombards probably account for a similar cluster of solidi found in the Rhineland. In the 580s Emperor Maurice sent 50,000 solidi to the Frankish king Childebert to expel the Lombards from Italy. Childebert, however, accepted the Lombards' submission himself and refused to repay the emperor. The presence of Byzantine gold in the Frankish world is well attested from finds as well as from the historical record. About a hundred gold and two hundred silver coins from the reign of Emperor Zeno (474–91), for example, have been found around the grave of Childeric (*c.* 457–81) at Tournai. This was an exceptional group, but nevertheless relates to what we know about the successor states' currency at that time. Since it was technically illegal to export the empire's coinage for trading purposes, it is likely that the bulk of Byzantine coins in the west originated in this sort of large-scale payment.

Many Byzantine gold coins would have been melted down to make ornaments and jewellery, and some were turned more directly into coin-jewellery or deposited as grave-goods to signify wealth and authority. However, the primary use of coin was still for currency. As well as utilizing eastern coin, the so-called 'barbarian' kings in the west issued their own, taking over this right just as they did so much of the machinery of late Roman government. The local coinages consisted of large (solidi) and smaller gold coins (tremisses), as well as lower denominations in silver and bronze. The designs of western coinage well illustrate the successor states' ambiguous relationship to the Byzantine emperor, generally following those of the imperial coinage. While some 'barbarian' rulers issued silver or bronze coins in their own names, their gold coins still continued to carry the name of the reigning eastern emperor, and the region's currency included a mix of Byzantine coins and local, so-called 'pseudo-imperial', issues, with the latter dominant. Many users of these coins would not have differentiated between them, and until the 7th century the coinage remained based on gold of the Byzantine standard.

'Pseudo-imperial' issues generally bear the current Byzantine emperor's image and name and the mint mark of Constantinople; differentiating them from genuine eastern issues has been a major task for numismatists. The Visigoths in Gaul in the 5th century (illus. 2) and in Spain in most of the 6th century struck gold solidi and tremisses in pseudo-imperial style, before beginning their own regal coinage about 580 and thereafter striking only tremisses. Similarly, the pseudo-imperial coinage of the Franks ran from roughly 500 to 587, although that of Provence continued until about 613.

The first exception to the issue of pseudo-

imperial coins is the gold coinage of the Frankish king Theodebert I (534–48), who extended his power into northern Italy in the 540s. Roman influence was prominent at his court and he was reportedly annoyed when he heard that Justinian I had assumed the victory name *Francicus*. As a sign of his political independence, he issued gold coins in his own name from his mint at Metz (illus. 3). Although the design remains a direct copy of the contemporary Byzantine gold solidus, some of his coins gave him titles strictly reserved for the emperor. This development angered the Byzantine authorities: the historian Prokopios, for example, described such coins as 'illegal' and 'presumptuous'. This coinage was not influential, however, and remained an anomaly

Left, top
**2. Gold solidus of the Visigoths in Gaul, in the name of Justinian I**
*Diam. 20mm; wt 4.38g*
*The British Museum, Department of Coins & Medals, 1855-2-13-38*

Left, bottom
**3. Gold coin of Theodebert I, Frankish king of Metz (534–48)**
*Diam. 20mm; wt 4.42g*
*The British Museum, Department of Coins & Medals, 1868-12-1-10*

Below
**4. Clay pilgrim's ampulla (oil flask) with St Menas, probably Egypt, 6th–7th centuries**
*H. 151mm; w. 109mm*
*The British Museum, Department of Prehistory & Europe, 1875-10-12-16*

for some time. Distinctive local coinages only developed significantly in the 570s and 580s, although among the Franks these coins mostly carried the name of the moneyer, and not that of the local king. Where the images of rulers were used, they still imitated Byzantine imperial style, which remained the basic physical manifestation of authority and power. These local coins were overwhelmingly of the small tremissis denomination. The large solidus remained almost a Byzantine monopoly, and examples are found in western coin hoards into the 640s, the latest such items seemingly being those of Emperor Heraklios.

Apart from high-level contacts, trade in several areas continued between Byzantine lands and the west, whether or not this was a major source in the transfer of coins to the west (there is little or no evidence of western coins moving to the east). Evidence of trade contacts is particularly strong for the Mediterranean coasts of France and Spain. The wreck of an early 7th-century ship known as Saint-Gervais 2, for example, found near the mouth of the Rhône in 1978, contained overwhelmingly eastern Mediterranean pottery, including pitchers with Greek graffiti. Eastern merchants were familiar in old Roman towns like Marseille, Bordeaux, Orléans, Seville and Cordoba. Another trade route seems to have operated from Italy across the Alps and up the Rhine to Frisia. Bulk products (oil, wheat, building materials) were involved just as much as the fine luxury items – especially silks and jewels – usually associated with the empire. Material came from Egypt as well as Syria and Constantinople, and finds in Europe of St Menas flasks (illus. 4), originating at the saint's shrine of Abu Mina in Egypt, show the pilgrim traffic that accompanied commerce.

## II. THE EDGE OF THE WORLD: BYZANTIUM AND BRITAIN

The island of Britain was at the fringes of the Roman and Byzantine worlds, and clear evidence of direct contact between Britain and the empire is ambiguous in the early middle ages. Nevertheless, there was certainly significant indirect contact, as networks of trade and diplomatic exchange still operated across the post-Roman world, bringing Byzantine material to Britain. In Constantinople, Prokopios' knowledge about ships trading from the Frankish lands to Thanet in Kent was presumably derived, directly or indirectly, from Byzantine sailors and merchants. It is possible that direct contact was maintained between Byzantium and the post-Roman, British kingdoms in the West Country and along the South Wales coast, the areas where quantities of Byzantine pottery and glass fragments, representing both tableware and storage vessels, have mostly been recovered.

New evidence is permitting a reappraisal of older opinions, since the discovery and recording of coins and other objects lost or deposited in 6th- and 7th-century Britain has increased dramatically with the advent of metal-detecting and the organized recording of this material introduced by the Portable Antiquities Scheme. Large quantities of Byzantine gold coinage reached the west in the form of imperial subsidies to allies and neighbours and through the pay of Byzantine armies. Some of this, mixed with western pseudo-imperial coins and local issues from Frankish, Visigothic and Burgundian regions, ended up being used in Britain, though doubtless much was melted down for reuse and some of it was turned into jewellery.

One of the most important pieces of coin-jewellery reusing a Byzantine coin is the Wilton Cross, discovered in Wilton, Norfolk (illus. 5). This is a cross-shaped gold and garnet *cloisonné* pendant set with a gold solidus of Emperor Heraklios, issued at Constantinople in 613–30. The coin was set with its reverse design (a cross potent on a stepped base) upside-down, perhaps so that it appeared the correct way up to the wearer when he or she raised it to their face. This and other fine examples of Anglo-Saxon

Left
**5. The Wilton Cross**
Cross-shaped gold and garnet cloisonné
Anglo-Saxon pendant, AD 675–700,
set with a gold solidus of Emperor
Heraklios (610–41); found in Wilton,
Norfolk, England
*H. 47mm; w. 45mm*
*The British Museum, Department of*
*Prehistory & Europe, 1859,5-12-1*

This page, top to bottom
**6. The Horndean hoard**

**a. Gold solidus of Emperor Honorius**
**(395–423)**
*Diam. 20mm; wt 4.47g*
**b. Gold solidus of Emperor Anastasius**
**(491–519)**
*Diam. 20mm; wt 4.5g*
**c. Gold solidus of Emperor Constans II**
**(641–68)**
*Diam. 18mm; wt 4.38g*
**d. Gold solidus of Emperor Constantine IV**
**(668–85)**
*Diam. 18mm; wt 4.25g*
*The British Museum, Department of Coins &*
*Medals, 1998-4-30-1-4*

7. Silver miliaresion of Emperor Heraklios
(610–41) from the Cuerdale hoard
*Diam. 22mm; wt 5.22g*
*The British Museum, Department of Coins &*
*Medals, loan from the Assheton Collection*

jewellery were probably made in an East Anglian workshop active in the early 7th century. Jewellery of similar workmanship was found with the Sutton Hoo graves in Suffolk, which also contained the finest assemblage of Byzantine silver plate ever found in western Europe. At least two other solidi of Heraklios turned into jewellery, if less grandly made, have been found in Britain.

Most of the imported coins were not reused in this way, however, and Byzantine coins have been found as part of the mixture of foreign gold coins across most of eastern England. More than thirty Byzantine gold coins of the 5th to 7th centuries have been recorded as single finds. These include four solidi, of the emperors Honorius (395–423), Anastasius (491–519), Constans II (641–68) and Constantine IV (668–85), all found in a field near Horndean, Hampshire; these may be either one hoard or single finds from a productive site (illus. 6). A definite hoard-find is the tremissis of Emperor Phokas from the crucially important mid-7th-century hoard from Crondall, Hampshire. Many more coins from Britain bear the name of Byzantine emperors of the period, but they are actually pseudo-imperial coins made in the west.

Material from important grave sites, notably Sutton Hoo (a uniquely rich source) and the Prittlewell burial in Essex, highlights the presence of Byzantine objects as a sign of status among the Anglo-Saxons. Other cemetery finds include a bronze censer from Glastonbury. This is one of more than thirty copper-alloy vessels known, mostly from Kent and East Anglia, but also from Oxfordshire,

8. Gold hyperpyron of Emperor Manuel I
Komnenos (1143–80), mint of
Constantinople
*Diam. 32mm; wt 3.7g*
*The Barber Institute Coin Collection,*
*B5692; P.D. Whitting Collection*

Dorset and the burial chamber at Taplow, Buckinghamshire. Out of the nine known examples of so-called Byzantine buckets (probably drinking vessels), three come from England (from the Isle of Wight, Hampshire and Suffolk). There are also finds of garnets, amethysts and ivory rings that originated in the eastern Mediterranean.

Thus, in early medieval Britain there was a reasonable degree of familiarity with genuine and imitative Byzantine coins. Some were adapted into jewellery and became decorative items alongside other prestigious objects that brought the empire's reflected glory to the local ruling elite. Even in the 8th century the great historian Bede cited Byzantine coinage as a benchmark for purity, comparing the virtue of a Kentish princess to 'the priceless and untarnished gold nomisma' (*aureum nomisma*).

Physical evidence of access to Byzantine material seems to fade in the 8th century. The only exceptions seem to have been connected with the onset of the Viking invasions in the late 9th century, with some Byzantine silver coins reaching Britain via Scandinavia as part of the large quantities of silver, mostly Islamic, derived from trade through the kingdom of Rus' along the river systems of central Europe and through the service of Scandinavian fighters in Byzantium. The huge Viking hoard from Cuerdale, Lancashire, deposited about 905, comprised almost 40 kilograms of silver objects, including an elderly double miliaresion of Heraklios (illus. 7). There seems to have been a revival of familiarity with Byzantine gold coins and other aspects of Byzantine culture in the 10th century, once the Viking threat briefly receded. Charters speak of *byzancteis nummi* and *nomismata auri*. Another indication of contact is King Athelstan's usage of the Byzantine title *basileus* – *totius Brittoniae basileus* (emperor of all Britain).

Contacts between Byzantium and the British Isles definitely revived between the 11th and 13th centuries. After the Norman Conquest many Anglo-Saxons took service with the Byzantine emperor, in part displacing Scandinavians as members of the Varangian Guard responsible for the emperor's personal safety. When participants in the First Crusade arrived in the eastern Mediterranean, they found a fleet of English (probably exiles from the Normans) already active there. The crusades brought many inhabitants of Britain to the eastern Mediterranean as crusaders or pilgrims, for some of whom Constantinople was a destination.

By the mid-12th century Byzantine gold coins were quite common in England, to judge from references to 'bezants' (the Latin word *bizantius* was used) in contemporary documents: this term appears to mean the hyperpyron of the later Komnenian and Angelan period, probably with issues of Manuel I Komnenos featuring significantly (illus. 8). So, in 1201 a young crusader, Robert Marsh, set off for the east with 20 marks in silver, 22 bezants, a gold ring, a horse, a helmet and sword and a cloak of scarlet. Bezants were also a source of gold for other ornaments, and in 1196 a cache of bezants was found in the workplace of a maker of gold cups, who presumably was intending to recycle them. They were particularly associated with ceremonies and royal power. The strong images of imperial authority they depicted had an impact on western royal imagery. Henry II, Richard I and Henry III are all recorded making gifts of bezants on important religious occasions. The presence of these coins reflected significant contact between Byzantium and England, particularly during Manuel I's reign, when Henry II received ambassadors in 1170 proposing a marriage alliance between Prince John and a Byzantine princess. Although this did not come about, several other Byzantine embassies visited Henry in the late 1170s.

### III. Rome, New and Old: Byzantium and Italy

Italy occupied a unique place for the Byzantine empire: Rome was the origin of its power, the Byzantines always regarded themselves as Roman by definition and, as head of the Christian empire, the emperor always took account of the pope. Italy was thus viewed as part of the empire, even though direct Byzantine control fluctuated significantly, until it disappeared for all practical purposes in the late 11th century. Even after this a substantial Greek-speaking population long continued to recognize the authority of the patriarch of Constantinople. Meanwhile the policies and intentions of Italian-based powers – Venice, the papacy, the western emperors, the kings of Sicily – remained fundamental for Byzantium and would prove to be a primary factor in its decline between the 13th and 15th centuries. The inevitable consequence was a deep level of contact and influence between the empire and Italy for as long as the former survived.

Although the Ostrogoths ruled Italy in the late 5th and early 6th centuries, the Byzantines were able to recover direct control under Justinian I, whose armies took Rome and Ravenna in 541. Byzantine Italy, however, was unable to withstand the Lombards, who entered Italy in 568 and took control of most of the north. They also created principalities in the south, the most important being Benevento, which controlled most of the region by the mid-8th century. The empire's influence survived only in parts of Apulia and Calabria, as well as Sicily. Nevertheless, these territories included such important cities as Naples and Amalfi, through which significant commerce was conducted, as well as through Venice in the north, which developed significantly in the 9th and 10th centuries. Byzantine Italy was ruled by an official called the exarch, based at Ravenna until its capture by the Lombards in 751. A number of cities, notably Venice, Rome and Naples, also continued to recognize the emperor's authority, if increasingly nominally. Sicily remained firmly under Byzantine authority until it was

captured by Arabs in 827. Despite serious attempts to recover the island, it remained in Arab hands until the Normans conquered it in 1091.

Byzantium's problem was that its interests in Italy usually had to give way before more fundamental threats to the empire's existence in the Balkans and the Middle East, although it remained a matter of concern. Emperor Constans II himself visited the pope in Rome in 662–3; at the time of his assassination at Syracuse, Sicily, in 668 it was rumoured he intended to make it the capital of the empire.

Unsurprisingly, the coinage of early medieval Italy was overwhelmingly influenced by that of Byzantium, though the level of influence fluctuated with the power and presence of its representatives and armies. The empire's own mints at Ravenna, Rome, Syracuse and some lesser places provided coins for the territories it controlled (illus. 9). In the 7th and 8th centuries the Byzantine coinage of Sicily was debased, but good gold from Constantinople was still available and it is this that is found in coin hoards from the time, presumably being put aside owing to its quality.

Top
**10. Gold tremissis of the Lombards,
in the name of Emperor Maurice**
*Diam. 16mm; wt 1.29g*
*The British Museum, Department of Coins
& Medals, BMC Lombards 23*

Bottom
**11. Silver siliqua of Emperor Leo III
(717–41) and Pope Gregory II,
mint of Rome**
*Diam. 7mm; wt 0.17g*
*The British Museum, Department of Coins
& Medals, 1993-5-28-6*

North Lombard coinage of the 7th century until about 680 consisted of pseudo-imperial gold tremisses in the name of the emperors Maurice (582–602), Heraklios (610–41) and Constans II (641–68), though they were not necessarily contemporary with them: it seems clear that coins in the name of Maurice, for example, were still being struck late in the 7th century (illus. 10). The Lombards meanwhile also received huge amounts of Byzantine coin, often from the exarch, to buy off their attacks; for several years this amounted to an annual tribute of 300 pounds of gold. The Lombards in the north did not strike solidi, perhaps because they had such large quantities of genuine Byzantine gold at their disposal – they certainly maintained the standards of their tremisses in a fixed relationship to Byzantine coinage.

From about 690 until the end of the Lombard kingdom in 774 there was a coinage in the name of the king, although a Byzantine-style coinage continued at Ravenna even after 751. The southern Lombards in Benevento, however, did strike solidi depicting themselves in the Byzantine style. This proved to be a point of cultural and political conflict in the late 8th century, when the Franks insisted that the Beneventan rulers should shave in the western style, rather than keep the beards and long hair common to both Byzantium and their own mythic ancestry as Lombards (Langobards: 'longbeards').

In Rome the popes gradually took over the authority of the dukes appointed by the emperor and began to issue a silver coinage of their own. Initially this retained an imperial bust on one side with a papal monogram on the reverse, for example pairing Leo III (717–41) with Pope Gregory II (715–31) (illus. 11). Byzantium's problems in defending Rome from the Lombards encouraged the popes to look to the powerful Frankish kings, whom they invited into Italy: Charlemagne conquered the Lombard kingdom in 774. The popes no longer formally recognized the Byzantine emperor as their lord by 781, when the emperor's regnal years stopped being used to date papal documents. After 800 the popes issued a joint coinage with the Carolingian emperors.

In the 9th and 10th centuries Byzantine involvement in Italy was based on a wary balance with its Carolingian, local and then Ottonian rulers. The scene would change dramatically in the 11th century, when Venice had become a powerful, independent force in the eastern Mediterranean and was able to

This page
**12. Silver grosso of Enrico Dandolo, Doge of Venice (1192–1205)**
*Diam. 19mm; wt 2.18g*
*The British Museum, Department of Coins & Medals, 1847-11-8-1440*

Next page
**13. The Borradaile Oliphant, ivory, southern Italy, late 11th century**
*L. 525mm*
*The British Museum, Department of Prehistory & Europe, 1923-12-5-3*

obtain important privileges for its merchants in Byzantine territory from Emperor Alexios I Komnenos (1081–1118). The kingdom of Sicily, newly created by incoming Normans at the expense of both the last surviving Byzantine territories in Italy and the Arabs in Sicily, was another hostile force. Both Venice and Sicily would be problematic for the empire's survival and had to be dealt with accordingly. It is ironic, but significant, that an important new coin based on Byzantine models was introduced into Venice in the shape of the grosso in about 1202 (illus. 12), just when the city was becoming increasingly hostile to the empire and shortly before it was instrumental in diverting the Fourth Crusade to Constantinople and shattering the empire's fabric.

The Norman kingdom of Sicily was built on hostility to Byzantium and its rulers always had designs on Byzantine territory across the Adriatic, an ambition continued by the Angevin dynasty that ruled Sicily from 1266. The culture of the Norman kingdom was a richly complex mixture of Lombardic, Byzantine, Frankish and Arab elements, as can be seen in such creations as the Borradaile Oliphant (illus. 13), a sounding horn made from an elephant tusk by a late 11th-century carver in southern Italy familiar with both Byzantine and Arabic traditions.

Norman coinage for the recently Byzantine mainland included the ducalis, introduced by King Roger II in 1140, and which in its design and concave nature was a copy of a trachy of Thessaloniki struck under Alexios I. It seems that Byzantine gold coinage remained an important element in the currency of both Venice and Sicily. It is likely that the preferred use of the hyperpyron was one reason why Venice, well behind its rivals Florence and Genoa, introduced its own gold coinage only after 1282, when the hyperpyron was debased from its established standard. In Sicily the augustale, a new western-style gold coin introduced by Frederick II in the 1240s, was still based on the hyperpyron in terms of its gold content, although its design is a deliberate echo of classical Roman coinage.

## IV. RIVALS OR PARTNERS? BYZANTIUM AND THE WESTERN EMPIRES

As Byzantine effectiveness in Italy declined, the popes looked to the Frankish kingdom, now the most powerful state in western Europe, to protect them from the Lombards. Charlemagne, king of the Franks, entered Italy in 774, conquered the

Lombards and became an Italian power. The Byzantines were conscious of this change and Empress Eirene negotiated a marriage alliance in 781 between Charlemagne's daughter Rotrud and her son, the young Emperor Constantine VI, to enhance their relations with the Franks, although the match was set aside in 787 as the two powers skirmished in Italy. In 800 Byzantium's relations with western Europe underwent a major change when Pope Leo III crowned Charlemagne Roman Emperor. One motive for this may have been the absence of a ruling male emperor from 797, with Eirene as ruling empress in Constantinople (illus. 14), although in 798 Charlemagne had in fact recognized Eirene's position. A marriage between Charlemagne and Eirene was briefly proposed as a solution to the diplomatic arguments that ensued. Between 804 and 810 the two empires were at war over the allegiance of Venice, before they came to a wary compromise and a Byzantine embassy visited Aachen.

Very few of Charlemagne's surviving coins carry the imperial title, and he probably used this on his coins only for the last two years of his reign, following his grudging recognition by the Byzantine emperor in 812. However, his son Louis the Pious, who succeeded him in 814, used the imperial title more consistently, as on a silver coin inscribed IMP AUG (Imperator Augustus, 'Emperor Augustus'), the normal imperial title on coins of the Roman Empire (illus. 15). The empire fragmented on Louis' death in 840 and was never fully reunited, although one branch always claimed seniority and the imperial title, retaining links with the east, as when Louis the

14. Gold solidus of Empress Eirene
(797–802), mint of Constantinople
*Diam. 20mm; wt 4.39g*
*The Barber Institute Coin Collection,*
*B4609; P.D. Whitting Collection*

Blind married Anna, the illegitimate daughter of Emperor Leo VI, in about 900.

When the Carolingian line in Germany became extinct, the imperial title fell into disuse for nearly forty years until a new dynasty headed by Henry I of Saxony and his son Otto I took power. Otto claimed the title of emperor, establishing what would eventually become the Holy Roman Empire of the Germans. Its leaders always sought coronation in Rome by the pope and regarded Italy as part of their domain. However, both Carolingian and Ottonian emperors usually accepted the status of the eastern empire, only wishing to obtain its collaboration and recognition. Rarely did they challenge its power directly, even in Italy, where both had interests, and diplomatic contact was reasonably frequent. Relations, however, could sometimes be difficult and the Byzantines were well aware of the significance of their monetary resources, as when an official of Nikephoros II remarked to Bishop Liutprand of Cremona, Otto I's delegate on a particularly uncomfortable mission: 'With the money in which we are strong we shall summon all nations against you and break you like a clay pot which, once broken, cannot be put together'.

The western and eastern empires, however, were increasingly cautious allies, especially when the presence of the Normans in southern Italy threatened to disrupt the traditional influence of both empires. These alliances often resulted in a Byzantine payment to their western ally, such as the subsidy of 144,000 nomismata paid to Henry IV in 1083 to obtain his assistance against the Normans in Sicily.

Between the 10th and 12th centuries a series of marriage alliances cemented this common interest, including Romanos II's betrothal to Bertha-Eudocia of Provence in 944, the marriage of the future Otto II to Theophano in 972 and that of Manuel I Komnenos to Bertha-Irene of Sulzbach in 1146, as well as the alliances that were proposed but never finalized. In about 950 Constantine VII conceded that the 'Franks' were the only foreigners whom a member of the Byzantine imperial family might marry, because Constantine the Great had ruled solely over the West at the beginning of his reign. All of these alliances were accompanied by sizeable dowries in cash: Theophano's dowry was immense and when Manuel I married his daughter to the king of Jerusalem in 1158, she brought with her the lavish sum of more than 100,000 hyperpyra in cash.

Byzantine influence on the Ottonian rulers was considerable. Eastern goods were simultaneously valued for their beauty and worth and distrusted as signs of luxury and pride. Surviving Byzantine artefacts and textiles – ivory plaques and boxes, gold and silver crosses and other religious ornaments, cameos, jewels, enamels, crystal chessmen, silks – demonstrate the movement of these goods into Ottonian Germany, either through trade or as high-level gifts. Many would have accompanied embassies and princesses, but some, such as small ivories, survive on a scale that suggests regular and extensive commerce. On the other hand, the confiscation of

silks from Liutprand of Cremona by hostile customs officials, as he returned from his embassy, suggests there was usually a strong political motive in their movement west. Byzantine-style objects manufactured for the Ottonian house, often in Italy, include an ivory plaque with images of Otto II and Theophano (illus. 16).

Byzantine crowns were an important gift and certainly influenced Ottonian practice, as coins bear witness. The coinage systems of east and west were now quite distinct, with that of the west based on the silver penny, and Byzantium's being a multi-metallic system using gold, silver and copper. Byzantine gold coins may have been utilized for high-value dealings and as offerings, as they were elsewhere in the west: contemporary documentary references show their presence in Germany, as in England and France, despite the lack of modern finds. The direct influence of Byzantine coinage on the forms of native western issues was, however, irregular but distinctive. Presumably the arrival of major payments of Byzantine coins had specific contemporary influences. Thus, in the 11th century the emperor is sometimes shown in a Byzantine crown with pendilia and one coinage from Speyer in the 1050s had both sides copied from the rare 1042 coinage of Zoe and Theodora: two figures holding a cross on one side and a facing bust of the Virgin with a medallion of Christ on her breast on the other (illus. 17).

# BYZANTIUM IN NORTHERN, CENTRAL AND EASTERN EUROPE

### I. SCANDINAVIA AND DENMARK

More than a thousand late Roman and Byzantine gold solidi have been found in the northern lands. The Swedish finds, both single coins and hoards, are mostly concentrated on three islands in the Baltic, in contrast to the large quantities of uncoined gold but few coins recorded from mainland Sweden. The coins are predominantly western issues from Rome and Ravenna between the mid-5th and mid-6th centuries. Coins found in Denmark and Norway are often looped or mounted and converted into jewellery. Their discovery raises interesting questions about the circumstances under which they reached Scandinavia, and their socio-economic impact on the local iron-age, non-monetary society. The dearth of archaeological evidence has led numismatists to speculate, basing their assumptions on die-studies, distribution patterns and statistics.

Among the more widely accepted theories are that the coins came from trade in wool between Scandinavia and the Romans, wages brought back by Scandinavian mercenaries, or from tribute money, originally paid to the Ostrogoths by the Romans and early Byzantines for their services or to ward off their attacks. Trade in furs between the Svear (Scandinavians) and the Romans, mentioned by Jordanes in his 6th-century history, offers another plausible explanation for the influx of gold coins. The fur trade leaves no remains, but Roman and Byzantine coined wealth seems to have had little impact on the local closed economy, and must have generated social imbalance rather than money exchange. The concealment of numerous coin hoards and the transformation of coins into jewellery, symbols of social status, support that argument.

By the 550s Scandinavians had reverted to their non-monetary economy, which remained the norm until the beginning of the Viking Age of the 9th and 10th centuries, when huge quantities of foreign silver coins, mostly Islamic dirhams, started arriving via Kievan Rus', due to trade in furs, spices and slaves. A relatively small quantity of Byzantine gold coins also arrived in the north, and testify to 9th-century contacts. Two interesting finds made during excavations at Haithabu/Hedeby in Schleswig are a nomisma of Theophilos (829–42) and the seal of a Byzantine official, the *patrikios* Theodosios. One solidus each of Constantine V (741–75) and Michael III (842–67) were included in a hoard from Norway dating to some time after 855, so the latter coin must have reached the north relatively soon after it was issued. Silver Byzantine coins appear to have made a

significant impact only in the late 10th century: miliaresia of Basil II and Constantine VIII, dating to *c.* 977 to 989, form half of all the Byzantine coins in the north. A local issue imitating this coinage was also struck at Sigtuna in Sweden about 1000 and other imitations of this coinage were made in Finland and Denmark, as well as perhaps in Kievan Rus'. Although these few hundred Byzantine examples are only a small proportion of the estimated 200,000 silver coins recovered from Viking Age Scandinavia, they may have had a larger significance in particular places and at particular times, as the imitative issues suggest.

In Denmark local coinage also became established around 1000. For the first half of the eleventh century designs were mostly derived from English coinage, which was then very common in Scandinavia, but Byzantine coins were also copied from the reign of Harthacnut (1035–42). One particularly interesting series of coins was struck at the mint of Lund by the moneyer Wulfet early in the reign of Sven Estridsen (1047–74). This has both a silver penny and the 'double penny' of King Sven, which copies the designs of a gold coin of Emperor Michael IV (1034–41), struck in 1041 and showing the emperor with the Archangel Michael on one side (illus. 18) and Christ on the other. These designs are combined on some coins or used together with an Anglo-Saxon design of a cross. Several other coins of Sven are direct imitations of Byzantine types, with designs including standing and seated figures of Christ, the Virgin and Child, and full-length figures and busts of an imperial-style monarch, all derived from coins from Constantinople.

A few gold coins of this period found in the north reinforce this Byzantine link, including two of Romanos III Argyros (1028–34) discovered in Sweden. Since there is extensive documentary evidence for the presence of considerable numbers of Byzantine gold coins in 12th-century England and France, although no actual finds have been made there in modern times, these Swedish finds and the influence of their designs on the Danish coinage suggest a significant Byzantine element in northern currency in the 11th century. Three imitations of the silver miliaresion of Constantine IX (1042–55) have also been found in Finland, indicating the presence in the area of Byzantine silver.

It has been suggested that gold Byzantine coins of this period may have been brought to Scandinavia by

Harald Hardrade ('Hardruler'), king of Norway (1047–66) and Sven's rival for the Danish throne. In the 1030s Harald had served in the Varangian Guard, the Byzantine emperor's bodyguard, and the Nordic sagas claim that he returned with a tremendous treasure, which he spent on pursuing his ambitions in Norway and Denmark. Byzantine coins were clearly present in some quantities in the north and had a definite influence on 11th-century Scandinavian coinage. Harald Hardrade was simply the most renowned figure among the large number of Norsemen who served in Constantinople in the late Viking Age.

## II. BYZANTINE EXPORTS TO EAST-CENTRAL EUROPE

Sixth-century Byzantine sources, archaeological remains and coin finds north of the river Danube trace Byzantium's earliest connection with east-central Europe, the lands now occupied by Croatia, Hungary, Poland, Romania, Slovakia and the Czech Republic. Abundant coin finds in that northern Byzantine frontier zone indicate the movement of armies, imperial envoys, merchants and possibly missionaries to areas controlled by the Avars by the second half of the sixth century. Byzantine merchants bought dairy products, animal skins, furs and slaves in exchange for wine, cereals, raw and processed iron, as well as luxury items. Subsidies, tribute money and ransoms for the liberation of prisoners of war also brought coins to that area. Subsidies were an expensive yet necessary measure in Byzantium's

relations with troublesome neighbours, and Justinian I (527–65) was happy to provide subsidies to the Avars and lobby them to attack other hostile tribes on his behalf. Yearly tribute was another considerable financial burden that added to Byzantium's dire economic situation in the late 6th century. The Avars' demand that Emperor Maurice (582–602) should increase his tribute payment from 80,000 to 100,000 gold solidi, and the emperor's refusal, was an explosive situation that led to the breakdown of the fragile peace treaty. The strategically located Byzantine cities of Sirmium (now Sremska Mitrovica) and Singidunum (now Belgrade) were lost to the Avars, who advanced across the Balkans as far as the Long Walls of Constantinople.

In 863 Byzantium's connection with east-central Europe acquired a different dimension when Rastislav, prince of Moravia, sent a request to Emperor Michael III (842–67) for a Christian missionary familiar with the Slavonic language. The Byzantine mission was led by the brothers Constantine (Cyril) and Methodios, two remarkable scholars from Thessaloniki, who were fluent in Slavonic. The Christianization of the Slavs in their own language, and the invention of the Glagolitic alphabet, the predecessor of the Cyrillic one, had far-reaching consequences. Through the transmission of Byzantine texts and spirituality a distinct Slavonic cultural identity and literary idiom were born, perceptively described by Michael III in his letter to Rastislav, cited in the *Life of Constantine*: 'Accept a gift greater and more precious than gold or silver or precious stones or transient riches…so that you may

**Top**
**19. Copper coin of Béla III, king of Hungary (1172–96)**
*Diam. 26mm; wt 3g*
*The Barber Institute Coin Collection, H62; E. Guest Bequest*

**Below, left**
**20a. Gold coin of Khan Omurtag (816–32)**
*Diam. 50mm; wt 2.742g*
*Archaeological Museum, Sofia, Bulgaria*

**Below, right**
**20b. Obverse of gold solidus of Emperor Nikephoros I (802–11), mint of Constantinople**
*Diam. 22mm; wt 4.4g*
*The Barber Institute Coin Collection, B4616; P.D. Whitting Collection*

also be numbered among the great nations that render glory to God in their own languages.'

The arrival of the Hungarians north of the Danube in the late 9th century opened a new chapter in the diplomatic, cultural and economic relations between Byzantium and central Europe. Although Hungary's prince Vajk, the future St Stephen (1000–38), placed his country in the spiritual sphere of the Roman Church, which promptly made him the first king of Hungary, Byzantine-Hungarian encounters remained important for both countries on many levels. Greek was used at the court of St Stephen, Byzantine monasteries and Byzantine-style churches were erected in his realm, diplomatic relations were twice sealed by marriage alliances and Hungarian armies fought alongside the Byzantines against the Seljuq Turks at the fateful battle of Myriokephalon (1176). Byzantine coins and jewellery from the 9th to the 12th centuries found north of the Danube have long been interpreted as signs of Byzantine monetary circulation, due to trade in salt between Magyars and Byzantines. The argument that they played an important role in the local economy, however, is undermined by the rarity of coin finds (mostly bronze) before the thirteenth century, their frequent presence in burials, and their use as pendants and amulets. Furthermore, archaeological evidence indicates that in the 10th and 11th centuries those areas experienced limited urbanization and hence a rather closed economy. Generalization of the monetary sector, based on the Carolingian system, must have begun in Hungary from the late 12th century and in Transylvania from the second half of the 13th. In a monetary system comprising silver deniers and bronze obols, finds of Byzantine folles can be seen as evidence of small change carried by travellers on their way to and from Byzantium, rather than of large-scale commercial activities.

The religious imagery of Byzantine coins, however, held a deep appeal, hence their use as pendants and amulets. Byzantine imagery also directly influenced the coinage of Béla III, king of Hungary (1172–96), reflecting the profound impact Byzantium had upon him during his ten-year stay in Constantinople at the court of Manuel I Komnenos (1143–80). His copper coins clearly follow Byzantine imagery and metrology (illus. 19) and Béla was himself to be remembered by his people as the 'Graecus' ('the Greek').

## III. Coinage and kingship in the medieval Balkans

Between the 7th and mid-11th centuries Bulgarian territories were subject to a closed economy, in which the use of coins was mostly geared towards trade in luxury goods with the Byzantines and was restricted to urban centres of administrative and commercial importance. The limited numbers of coins that entered monetary circulation were initially Byzantine issues, mostly gold, supplemented in the 10th and 11th centuries by local imitations of Byzantine gold coins in gilded bronze and gold, and cast copies of Byzantine anonymous folles A1 [970–76(?)] and A2 [976(?)–c. 1030/35]. The earliest known Bulgarian coins are two gold specimens from the reign of Khan Omurtag (816–32) found in excavations near Varna and Veliko Turnovo. They are both struck on only one side and there has been a long debate as to whether they were intended as seals, medallions or coins. Whether one accepts them as presentation coins or seals, it is extraordinary how the Bulgarian khan, a pagan and fierce persecutor of Christians, chose to be depicted. Omurtag's image is based on that of Emperors Nikephoros I (802–11) and Leo V (813–20) on their Constantinopolitan gold coins (illus. 20). Dressed as a Byzantine emperor, Omurtag carries a cross-topped sceptre and an *akakia*. The accompanying inscription, written in a mixture of Greek and Latin characters, presents the khan to the coinage's intended recipients: *Khan, Soubegi* [equivalent of emperor] *Omurtag*.

Imagery and inscriptions on ancient and medieval

coins were an important component in the expression and exercise of power, and in that respect the coins of Omurtag are among the most obvious physical manifestations of medieval Bulgaria's encounter with Byzantine ideas of kingship. Byzantine imperial titles were to fascinate Bulgarian rulers. Tsar Symeon was the first to adopt the title Emperor of the Romans in the 920s and his son Peter modelled his seals after contemporary Constantinopolitan gold coins, adopting the title Emperors of the Bulgarians for himself and his Byzantine royal bride.

In the later medieval Balkans, Bulgarian coinage remained the closest to Byzantine examples in its choice of imagery, inscriptions, monetary values and striking techniques. Between 1195 and 1230 Bulgaria's monetary system consisted mostly of

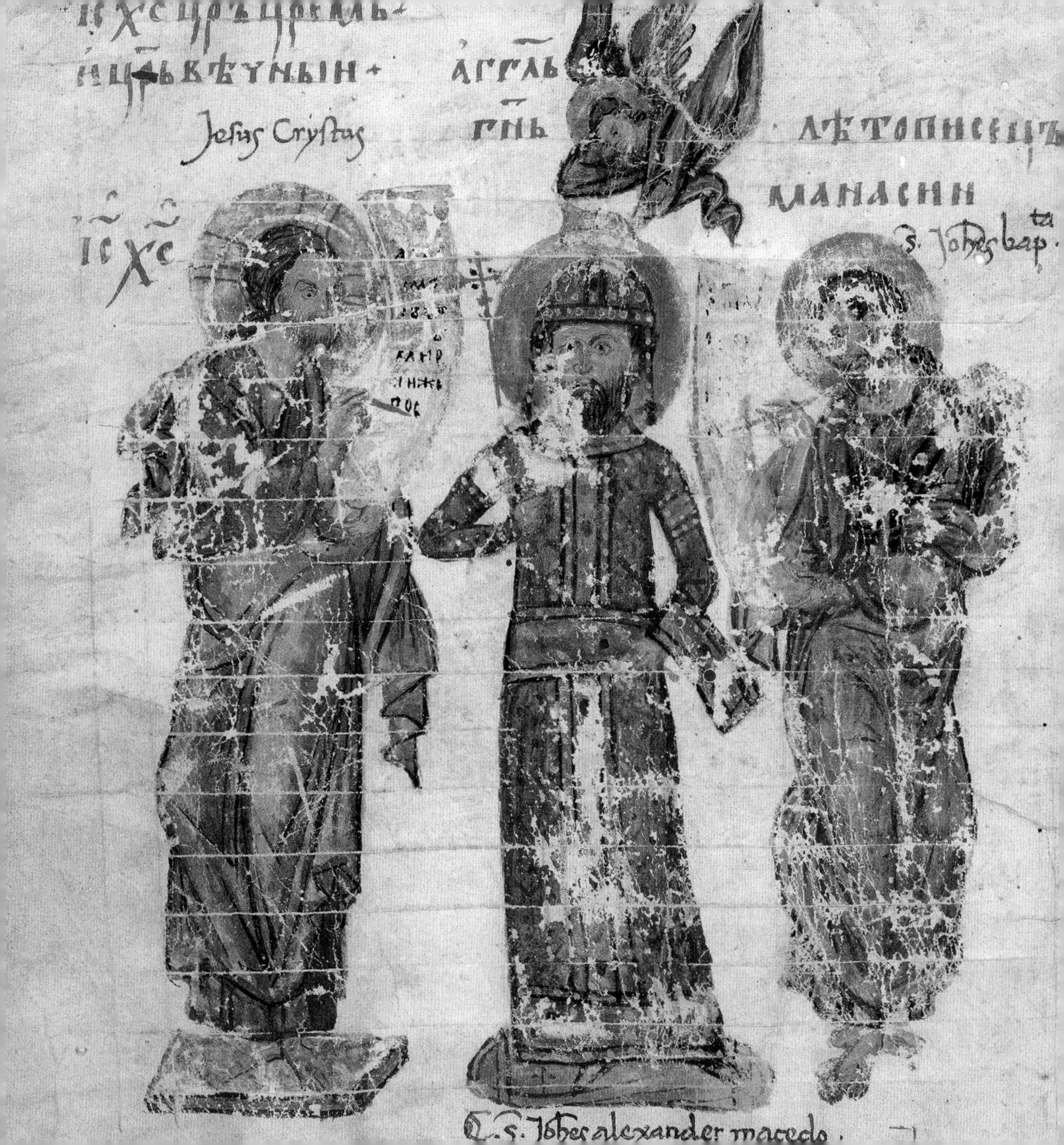

billon trachea. A limited series of gold hyperpyra primarily served a political purpose rather than being intended for monetary circulation. The elegant hyperpyra and billon trachea of Tsar Ivan Asen II (1218–41) are an excellent example of the use of coins as political instruments. Struck after his victory against the Byzantines at Klokotnitza, they were modelled on contemporary Byzantine coins from the mints of Thessaloniki and Nicaea, and reflect the Bulgarian tsar's political ambitions to rule over Greeks and Bulgarians, as his title (Tsar of the Bulgarians and the Greeks) appropriately suggests (illus. 21). The presence of St Demetrios, Thessaloniki's patron saint, in the company of Ivan Asen II on the coins adds to the political message the tsar wants to convey. Demetrios is now seen as one of the patron saints of the Assenid dynasty, having allegedly migrated from Thessaloniki in 1185 to the capital of medieval Bulgaria, Turnovo, described in an interpolation to the 14th-century Old Bulgarian translation of the Byzantine Manasses chronicle as a new Rome (illus. 22).

In neighbouring Serbia the oldest coinage is that of Kral Stefan Radoslav (1228–34). Modelled on contemporary Byzantine coins, Stefan Radoslav's electrum and billon trachea differ significantly from later Serbian coins in their shape, size, Greek inscriptions and iconography. As Theodore Komnenos Doukas' son-in-law, the Serbian kral echoes in his coinage aspects of Byzantine imperial ideology. On the reverse of his billon trachea (an alloy of silver and copper) he is depicted in the company of St Constantine, in line with coins of Emperor Alexios III (illus. 23). The accompanying inscriptions in Greek on his coins attribute to him the impressive titles of King (*Rex*), Duke (*Doux*) and Emperor (*Autokrator*). Is this a mere copy of a Byzantine prototype, created in the mint of Thessaloniki? Archaeological evidence from the medieval capital city of Ras (its remains lie near the city of Novi Pazar) suggests that these coins were most likely struck in Serbia. Apart from demonstrating economic planning and the need for monetary transactions, Stefan's coins also reflect the adoption of Byzantine and western royal titulature.

Between the 13th and 15th centuries Serbian coinage adopted a much more western outlook in the choice of metallic values and coin designs. Venetian grossi circulated widely in the western Balkans and Serbian dinars, made possible through the opening of new silver mines in Serbia, were modelled on contemporary western silver coins. However, Byzantine imperial ideology remained an important aspect of Serbian coinage. The political ambitions and expansionist policy of Stefan Dusan (1331–55) are encapsulated in the Latin inscriptions that surround his image on some of his silver coins: King (*Rex*) of Raska (*Rasie*) and Emperor (*Imperator*) of the Romans (*Romanorum*).

Imagery and inscriptions on medieval Balkan coins formulated, in an abbreviated yet clear manner, political ideas that developed at the crossroads of east and west. Coin inscriptions identify rulers as tsars, krals, emperors, despots, or even emperors of the Greeks and Bulgarians, or of the Romans. The grand idea of the imperial office is dressed in either

**23. Billon trachy of King Stefan Radoslav (1228–34), mint of Ras**
Obv. Christ seated upon throne/Rev.
Standing facing figures of the king and
St Constantine holding between them a
patriarchal cross on a long shaft.
*Diam. 28mm; wt 2.92g*
*The Barber Institute Coin Collection, 2-2006;*
*The Henry Barber Trust; the 'Friends' of*
*the Barber Institute Fund*

Byzantine or western fashion, and the proliferation of one or another iconographical motif reflects the various political agendas held by Balkan rulers, the audiences they were addressing, and the impact of Byzantine and western currencies on the local monetary systems. Images look strikingly similar, which perhaps says much about communications and the movement of ideas, coin dies and die-engravers in the later medieval Balkans.

## IV. Tradition and innovation: the case of Russia

The first coinage of the Rus' in the late 10th century emerged after a Russo-Byzantine marriage alliance and the official encounter of Kievan Rus' with Orthodox Christianity, imperial ideology and culture. Byzantium's appeal proved enduring and in the late 15th century Russian theologians would claim that Moscow was now the new Constantinople, the third Rome, destined never to fall.

Before the 10th century Rus' monetary economy was served mostly by Islamic dirhams and western European deniers, found in great numbers as single finds and in coin hoards. The limited presence and diffusion of Byzantine coins, on the other hand, seems to have been mostly concentrated in and around the Crimean peninsula and the Byzantine outpost of Cherson. All this was to change in 988. Prince Vladimir's conversion to Christianity and his marriage to the Byzantine princess Anna, sister of Emperor Basil II (976–1025), brought a new era in

Russia's religious and cultural development, and in its relations with Byzantium. The bridegroom was to be baptised in St Basil's church in Cherson, to give the city back to the Byzantines as a marriage gift to Anna, and to assist his Byzantine brother-in-law with troops to help suppress the rebellion of Bardas Phokas. The marriage alliance also led to an influx of Byzantine clergy, whose mission was the mass baptism of the Rus' and the maintenance of Anna's Constantinopolitan life and style of worship in her new home city, Kiev. A magnificent church dedicated to the Mother of God was commissioned by Vladimir and executed by Byzantine builders. This offered the Russian prince further association with the Orthodox faith and Byzantine imperial ideology. The best reflection of Vladimir's new image as a powerful Orthodox ruler can be found in his coinage. His zlatniki (gold coins) and srebreniki (silver coins) are modelled on contemporary Byzantine issues, with some modifications necessary to cater to Vladimir's taste and needs. The facing bust of Christ Pantokrator on the obverse of his earlier coins copies that on the gold histamena and tetartera of Basil II. The reverse imagery exalts the newly baptised Christian ruler, who is shown enthroned, dressed in Byzantine fashion, wearing a Byzantine crown and holding a cross-topped sceptre and a trident (illus. 24). The latter, an old symbol of authority in the house of Vladimir, offers the connection with his own heritage. Later issues reflect innovations in the use of style, symbols and inscriptions: the obverse image of Christ gives way to the trident-like device, while the reverse shows the enthroned ruler nimbate

24. Silver coin of Vladimir I (988–1015), mint of Kiev
*Diam. 27mm; wt 2.24g*
*The Fitzwilliam Museum, Cambridge,*
*Department of Coins & Medals;*
*Philip Grierson Collection (PG 11,828)*

and surrounded by the inscription 'Vladimir, and this is his gold' on the gold coins, and 'Vladimir, and this is his silver' on the silver ones. Coins of Vladimir's successors demonstrate iconographic links with Byzantine seals, thus reflecting the movement of merchants and officials in Russian lands. The figures of St Peter and St George on the reverse of srebreniki issued by Svyatopolk I (1015–17, 1018–19) and Yaroslav I (1019–54), respectively, are to be found on 11th-century Byzantine ecclesiastical seals, and the same applies for the Greek word AMHN (Amen) on the obverse of Russian coins.

The influence of Byzantine coinage and cultural traditions lasted well after the 11th century, as Byzantium remained for Russians the ideal Christian empire and a steady point of cultural reference, despite the increasing hardship experienced by Byzantium. Commercial relations continued until late and, even when trade routes became dominated by western merchants, pilgrims continued to flock to Constantinople, vividly describing the city's topography and marvels in the 14th and 15th centuries. An account composed by Ignatii of Smolensk, a monk, must have been responsible for a coronation custom transplanted in an interesting fashion to Russia. Ignatii left Ryazan for Constantinople in spring 1389, and his pilgrim's itinerary is a fascinating description of the route

south along the Don river to the Black Sea and the Mediterranean. During his stay in Constantinople he witnessed the coronation of Manuel II in the church of Hagia Sophia, after which, according to his diary, 'as [the emperor] left the church he was showered with stavrata which all the people tried to grab with their hands'. Either Ignatii misunderstood the old tradition of distributing bags of coins to the people upon the emperor's coronation, or he witnessed a 14th-century innovation. In the light of a contemporary Byzantine coronation protocol that correctly describes the ritual, the idea that the emperor was showered with coins seems rather unlikely, or implies the introduction of a foreign ritual in the late Byzantium ceremonial. A contemporary Genoese account which also talks of Genoese officials scattering coins over the head of Manuel's bride upon her arrival in Constantinople could support the latter hypothesis. Whatever might have been the reason for Ignatii's slightly different description, his account seems to have established a Russian ritual of throwing coins to the newly crowned ruler. Ivan III, when crowning his grandson Dimitri Ivanovic as co-ruler in 1498, showered him with gold and silver coins, and in 1547 at the first Muscovite imperial coronation of Ivan IV, which was faithfully modelled on the Byzantine ritual, the newly crowned tsar was duly showered with gold and silver coins as he left the church.

Byzantium in northern, central and eastern Europe

# BYZANTIUM'S EASTERN NEIGHBOURS: COINAGE AND LEGITIMACY

In the eastern Mediterranean coins and seals, more than any other art medium, reflect profound changes at the socio-economic and political level and the complex relations between the medieval east and west.

In a climate of cultural and linguistic symbiosis, Arab, Seljuq, Turkmen, Mongol and Ottoman rulers, Georgian and Armenian kings, and the emperors of Trebizond used coinage as a mirror reflecting their relation with the past and their political aspirations for the future. Ideas of legitimacy, continuity and permanence are dressed in Byzantine, oriental and western fashion, and the use of particular images and inscriptions indicates the various connections the rulers were seeking and the different audiences they were addressing. Images look similar, and at times transposed, with Georgians and Armenians using Islamic motifs and Arabic script, and with Arab and Turkish princes, later including sultan Mehmet II, drawing inspiration from Byzantine, Roman and Hellenistic iconography.

## I. Byzantium and the Islamic world

### a. Early Islamic coinage: the Byzantine and Sasanian legacy

About 600 the lands that later became the Ottoman empire were under the cultural influence of two main powers: Byzantium controlling the Mediterranean, and the Sasanians ruling the areas today covered by Iran and Iraq. By the mid-7th century the Arabs had defeated the Byzantines in Syria and Egypt and overthrown the Sasanians, and by the early 8th their conquests stretched from Spain to India.

Byzantine coins were first used and then imitated (illus. 25) by the Islamic administration of the conquered areas. The symbol of the cross was removed from both the obverse and reverse, while the traditional Latin inscription that refers to the cross (Victory of the Emperors) was replaced by the *shahada* in Kufic surrounding a pole on steps: 'In the name of God, there is no God but Allah, he is alone, Muhammad is his prophet'.

In the east Muslims followed the Sasanian model in the production of their silver dirhams, which in turn prompted 8th-century production of Byzantine silver miliaresia. The image of a ruler and the Zoroastrian fire-altar depicted on Sasanian drachms was maintained on Islamic dirhams, but supplemented by the appropriate inscription *bissmilah* (In the name of God), and by the Islamic governor's name. The Sasanian legacy lasted long after the reform of the Islamic coinage in AH 77 (AD 696) and influenced the development of circulating currency across the eastern Mediterranean.

Top
**25a. Obverse of gold solidus of Emperor Heraklios (610–41), mint of Constantinople**
*Diam. 21mm; wt 4.4g*
*The Barber Institute Coin Collection, B2916; P.D. Whitting Collection*

Bottom
**25b. Obverse of gold dinar of Caliph Abd al-Malik (AD 685–705), probably struck at Damascus, c. 691–2**
*Diam. 19mm; wt 4.4g*
*The Barber Institute Coin Collection, A-B30; P.D. Whitting Collection*

## b. Looking for Alexander, 11th–15th centuries

An amazing array of images, both secular and religious, appeared on the coinage of Muslim rulers of Anatolia between the 11th and 14th centuries, drawing on the area's distant pre-Islamic past as well as more recent and contemporary motifs encountered in the Byzantine and Crusader coinage of the eastern Mediterranean.

Among the coins, 12th-century copper dirhams created by the Artuqids of Mardin, which copy 2nd-century BC silver tetradrachms of Antiochos VII (illus. 26), have traditionally been viewed in the light of the Artuqids' antiquarian interest. More than an expression of antiquarian or astrological fascination, this coin type and a host of similar ones displaying portraits of Hellenistic, Roman (illus. 27) and

Top, left

**26a. Obverse of copper dirham of Najm al-Din Alpi, Artuqid ruler of Mardin (AH 547–72, AD 1152–76)**
*Diam. 28mm; wt 13g*
*The Barber Institute Coin Collection, TK359; P.D. Whitting Collection*

Top, right

**26b. Silver tetradrachm of Antiochos VII Euergetes (138–129 BC)**
*Diam. 28 mm; wt 16.4g*
*The Barber Institute Coin Collection, G29*

Bottom, left

**27a. Obverse of copper dirham of Qutb al-Din II-Ghazi II, Artuqid ruler of Mardin (AH 572–80, AD 1176–84)**
*Diam. 32mm; wt 9.8g*
*The Barber Institute Coin Collection, TK45; P.D. Whitting Collection*

Bottom, right

**27b. Obverse of gold solidus of Constantine the Great (303–37), mint of Nicomedia**
*Diam. 21mm; wt 4.5g*
*The Barber Institute Coin Collection, R3095; P.D. Whitting Collection*

Byzantine rulers (illus. 28) need to be considered as part of the Turkish rulers' overall quest for continuity and legitimacy. The portrait of Antiochos belongs to a long iconographical tradition introduced by Lysimachos (323–281 BC), one of Alexander the Great's generals. Idealized portraits of Alexander and realistic portraits of his Hellenistic successors provided a model for the ruler's portraiture of the late Roman republican and imperial coinage. Later developments in Byzantine coinage shifted attention from Hellenistic ideals to the Christian image of the emperor. Hellenistic and Roman portraits re-emerge, however, on Islamic coins of medieval Anatolia. The choice presents no paradox, for in the late medieval eastern Mediterranean the image of Alexander was part of the arts and literature created by Westerners, Byzantines, Armenians and medieval Muslims (illus. 29). For Turkish princes, Alexander's conquest of the world and search for wisdom belonged to the fabric of heroic and narrative poetry developed for the Islamic élites in Persia and Anatolia, and in that respect imagery related to him and inscriptions referring to Turkish dominion over the east evoked continuity.

After the fall of Constantinople, a late 15th-century medal commissioned by Mehmet II concludes that long quest for legitimacy. Executed by Bertoldo di Giovanni (illus. 30), it offers a realistic portrait of an ageing and pensive Mehmet II on the obverse, while on the reverse the sultan's triumph follows the iconography of Roman coins and medals. The intriguing issue is not what the Italian master had in mind and his sources of imagery, but the intended fusion between East and West. A youthful and svelte sultan, in the manner of Alexander and Augustus, who never aged in their numismatic portraits, appears riding a chariot, at the back of which three naked and bound females, all wearing crenellated crowns, represent Asia, Greece and Trebizond. Mars, the god of war, leads the triumph, while Mehmet holds high in his left hand a small Victory, in line with Roman imperial iconography. This extraordinary medal formulates in the most eloquent way the end of a long pursuit. Mehmet II is, as the obverse and reverse inscriptions state, the emperor of Asia, Trebizond and even Magna Graecia, the latter title indicating Mehmet's designs on the kingdom of Naples. He is also shown as the latest addition in an uninterrupted line of rulers leading back to Alexander.

### c. Faces of Islam: Visualizing Maryam, Christ and Jibrâ'îl

Another extraordinary element in Islamic coins struck in medieval Anatolia is the inclusion of religious imagery customarily associated with Christian iconography. Images of the Virgin Mary, Christ, the Archangel Gabriel and St John the Baptist adorn copper dirhams and imitative florins and gigliati struck in the realms of Artuqid and Seljuq rulers, copying Byzantine, Florentine, Neapolitan and Venetian coins that circulated in the area. The Virgin Mary figures prominently in Islam, being regarded by Muhammad as the highest woman in all creation. Her purity, exceptional qualities and role in the history of mankind are underlined by Muhammad, who by understanding Christ solely as the son of Mary, *Issa ibn Maryam*, rejects Christ's divine nature.

**Top**

**30. Bronze medal of Sultan Mehmet II (1451–81) by Bertoldo di Giovanni, c. 1480**

*Diam. 93mm*

*The British Museum, Department of Coins & Medals, 1919-10-1-1*

**Centre**

**31. Gold histamenon of Emperor Romanos III (1028–34), mint of Constantinople**

*Diam. 25mm; wt 4.4g*

*The Barber Institute Coin Collection, B5530; P.D. Whitting Collection*

**Bottom, left**

**32. Obverse of copper dirham of Fakhr al-Din Qara Arslan, Artuqid ruler of Hisn Kayfa (AH 539–70, AD 1144–74)**

*Diam. 29mm; wt 7.3g*

*The Barber Institute Coin Collection, TK434; P.D. Whitting Collection*

**Bottom, right**

**33. Reverse of copper dirham of Najm al-Din Alpi, Artuqid ruler of Mardin (AH 547–72, AD 1152–76)**

*Diam. 32mm; wt 16.1g*

*The Barber Institute Coin Collection, TK368; P.D. Whitting Collection*

The unique position that Mary enjoyed in the Islamic and Christian communities of Anatolia provided Turkish princes with the right platform to countermark 11th-century Byzantine folles that bore her image, and eventually to create their own version of Mary on their copper dirhams of the second half of the 12th century (illus. 33).

The image of Christ, based on Byzantine prototypes (illus. 31), was chosen by the Turkish rulers of Kayfa, Sivas, Aleppo and Diyarbakır for some of their coin designs (illus. 32). As with Marian iconography, images of Christ on contemporary Islamic coins should not be viewed as bizarre or accidental. The Qur'an accepts Jesus Christ as one of the prophets, the messenger of God, and as the 'Word' of God without definition, 'created like Adam'. This concept, in combination with the religious beliefs and prehistory of most of the population that handled Byzantine, Crusader and Islamic coins in Anatolia, must have shaped quite a permissive climate in which Christ played an important role in Muslim life, just as Muhammad started infiltrating the beliefs of Anatolian Christians through the teaching of Rumi. By creating currencies similar in weight and iconography to established ones, Turkish princes successfully addressed different religious and cultural audiences living and paying taxes in their realms.

A winged figure depicted on some Artuqid coins is also important (illus. 34). The imagery draws on two different sources, the Victory on Roman imperial coins and depictions of angels and the Archangel Gabriel in Christian and Islamic art. Venerated by Muslims as the messenger of God and known as

34. Obverse of copper dirham of Nur al-Din Muhammad, Artuqid ruler of Hisn Kayfa (AH 571–81, AD 1175–85)
*Diam. 28mm; wt 14.6g*
*The Barber Institute Coin Collection, TK1;*
*P.D. Whitting Collection*

Jibrâ'îl in the Qur'an, Gabriel acquires visual form in Anatolia's medieval Islamic art with a few necessary changes from his Byzantine depictions. A superb example of this effortless transformation is an elegant 6th-century Constantinopolitan marble relief, once gracing a Christian place of worship in the area of Antalya. Rather than being disfigured or destroyed by the Seljuqs, it was reused in the course of the 13th century. Gabriel became Jibrâ'îl with the simple addition of the word *Allah* in the medallion the Archangel was originally holding.

## II. Byzantium's Christian neighbours: Georgia and Armenia

### a. 4th–11th centuries

East of the Black Sea, Armenia and Georgia held the often uncomfortable position of buffer zones between Byzantium and the east. Positioned at the crossroads of major interregional routes, both kingdoms remained meeting places for people, commodities and ideas, experiencing commercial activity and invasions alike.

In the mid-5th century the Armenian Church embarked on a path of autonomy, shaping a distinct character for the country's religion, language and sense of identity that led to independence and prosperity under the Bagratid dynasty from the late 9th century. The arrival of Seljuq Turks in Asia Minor by the mid-11th century drove many Armenians south-west, towards the Taurus mountains and close to the Mediterranean, where they founded the kingdom of Cilician or Lesser Armenia.

In Georgia, meanwhile, Orthodoxy ensured a mostly uninterrupted bond with Byzantium, and between the 6th and 11th centuries Georgians and Byzantines fought the Sasanians and the Arabs. The political, socio-economic and religious presence of different cultural groups in the area is best reflected in the multitude of currencies that circulated in Georgia's territories. Between the 5th and 7th centuries Byzantine coinage was the main circulating medium in western Georgia (Lazica in Byzantine sources), while silver Sasanian drachms remained the standard currency in Sasanian-dominated eastern Georgia.

The start of eastern Georgia's independence is marked by the first coinage struck by local rulers (*erismtavars*). Hybrid Georgian-Sasanian silver drachms, modelled after their Sasanian counterparts, cleverly combined elements of both religions, substituting the Christian cross for the sacred flame depicted on the Zoroastrian fire-altar of Sasanian coins. Monograms of *erismtavars* were later replaced by their full names in Georgian script.

The capture by the Arabs of eastern Georgia and its capital, Tbilisi, in the 7th century opened a new chapter in Georgia's history. Tbilisi grew as an important trade centre, and currencies changing hands in its market ranged from Islamic to Byzantine coins. Byzantine coin finds are not only related to commercial interchange, but also to the presence of Byzantine armies in the 8th century, which, joined by Khazars and Abkhazians, defeated the Arabs at Anakopia. The independent kingdom of Egrisi-Abkhazian was born. Georgian coinage mirrors most

**35. Copper coin of King David IV of Georgia (1089–1125)**
*Diam. 34mm; wt 10.82g*
*The British Museum, Department of Coins & Medals, 1857-12-26-7*

eloquently the country's development from client state in the Byzantine orbit to independent kingdom. Silver coins struck at the end of the 10th century by David III follow Byzantine miliaresia in weight and quality; their reverse inscription commemorates the title of *kuropalates* bestowed upon David by Emperor Basil II in 979. Silver coins struck by Bagrat IV (1027–72) and Giorgi II (1072–89) are an interesting combination of Byzantine iconography and Greek inscriptions on the obverse, with the name and title of the king in Georgian script on the reverse. The obverse image of the Virgin Blachernitissa follows 11th-century Byzantine prototypes, while the reverse inscription states the name of the king and the people over of whom he rules. He is the king of the Abkhazians and Kartleans, and also *nobilissimos* or *sebastos* in relation to the Byzantine emperor. It is only on the copper coins of David IV the Builder (1089–1125) that the Georgian king appears equal to his Byzantine counterpart. He is shown on the obverse dressed in Byzantine imperial attire, wearing stemma, and holding a globus cruciger (illus. 35), and the accompanying inscription in Georgian refers to him simply as King David. On the reverse an invocation in Georgian surrounding a cross lists the extent of David's kingdom: 'Lord aid David, king of Abkhazians, Kartvelians, Ranians, Kakhetians, Armenians'.

An important marriage alliance between Byzantium and Georgia left its mark in contemporary literature and art (illus. 36) when King Bagrat IV gave his daughter in marriage to Emperor Michael VII Doukas (1071–8). The Georgian bride, famous for her beauty, intelligence and wisdom, is a rare example of a Byzantine empress shown on coins. She first appears on Michael's gold tetartera and silver miliaresia, and after 1078 on the miliaresia of Nikephoros III Botaneiates (1078–81) following his usurpation and marriage with Maria. Her bust and name next to that of Nikephoros is a clear indication of the legitimacy the usurper was seeking through marriage with the empress. Are these coins the last reminder of Maria's presence in the life of the empire? In 1994 excavation of a monastic complex on Mount Papikion, a renowned late Byzantine monastic centre in western Thrace, unearthed a tomb empty but for a golden seal ring (illus. 37). Like Mount Athos, Mount Papikion was an *abaton*, a place where no women were allowed. But the ring clearly belonged to a woman whose remains were once buried there and later transported to their final resting place; silver threads remaining from her garments indicate her wealth and importance. The letters MARIA BOTONIATINA

on the ring identify it as belonging to the wife of Nikephoros Botaneiates. Maria owned estates in Christoupolis (Kavala), Pernikos (Pernik) and in the kastron of Petritzos on the northern slopes of the Rhodope mountains, and she was an important benefactor to the monastery of Iviron at Mount Athos. It seems that the monastic complex on Papikion, possibly one of Maria's foundations, became the Georgian princess's penultimate resting place.

### b. 11th–15th centuries

The arrival of Seljuq Turks in the 11th century dramatically changed the political geography of the area and shaped the form, iconography and language used in the currencies produced by Anatolian Christians.

Cilician Armenia, a major communication hub, flourished as a trading and cultural centre until it fell to the Mamelukes of Egypt in 1375. Its coinage, which developed amidst Crusader states, Turkish-controlled areas and in the context of economic relations with Byzantium and the west, included

Previous spread

**36. An 11th-century marriage alliance between Byzantium and Georgia**

**a. Reverse of gold tetarteron of Michael VII Doukas (1071–8), mint of Constantinople**
*Diam. 30mm; wt 4.01g*
*The Barber Institute Coin Collection, B5460;*
*P.D. Whitting Collection*

**b. The coronation of Michael VII and Maria.**
**Enamel panel, part of the Khakhuli icon**
*State Art Museum, Tbilisi, Georgia*

Above

**37. Gold seal ring of Empress Maria, 11th century**
Found during archaeological work in a
monastic complex, Mount Papikion,
Western Thrace, 1994
*12 Ephorate of Byzantine Antiquities,*
*Kavala, Greece*

gold, silver and copper coins. Apart from a few bilingual coins in Armenian-Arabic script and some others in Latin characters, the majority of inscriptions on Cilician Armenian coins are in Armenian, while their iconography looks both east and west for inspiration.

Seljuq raids in the second half of the 11th century devastated Georgia, gradually turning the land to pasture and ruining the region's economy. After a stage of vassalage to the Turks, Georgian kings fought back. Under Queen Tamar (1184–1213) and Giorgi IV Lasha (1213–23) Georgia's frontiers expanded to the north and south, encompassing a multiethnic population. Art and literature reached their peak, and grand building projects in Gelati and Vardzia celebrated a period of optimism and prosperity. But Georgia's golden age was cut short by the arrival of the Mongols in 1223. The subsequent fragmentation of the Georgian kingdom, its economic decline due to heavy financial obligations to the Mongols, and the depopulation of the country following the Black Death (1366) and Timur's invasions in 1386 prepared the ground for the gradual submission of Georgia to Turks and Iranians.

On the northeast coast of Anatolia, the empire of Trebizond, founded by David and Alexios I Komnenos (1204–22), members of the homonymous Byzantine imperial family, survived Turkish attacks, civil wars and domestic intrigues until 1461, when it was annexed by the Ottomans. One of the successor states following the fall of Constantinople to the Latins in 1204, Trebizond remained independent from Byzantium even after the recovery of Constantinople in 1261, but was often forced to pay tribute to its Muslim neighbours.

## c. Between East and West

Christian rulers in Anatolia chose different ways to be depicted on their coins, each fashion being a mere reflection of political statements, alliances or vassalage.

Cilician Armenian kings are shown seated on a throne adorned with lion heads, and holding a fleur-de-lis. Their overall posture and the presence of the fleur-de-lis follow contemporary western motifs and echo the connection between Cilician Armenia and the west through religion, political arrangements, trade and intermarriage.

Rulers on horseback on Cilician Armenian coins, Trebizond aspra and their Georgian imitations are another iconographical innovation, drawing inspiration primarily from the Persian court ethos and art, Seljuq coins and, to a lesser extent, from coins and seals of the Latin east. The connection with the Seljuqs is obvious on silver trams of Hetoum II (1289–1305), king of Cilician Armenia, the reverse inscriptions of which are in Arabic and refer to the sultans of Konya, Kaykobad and later Kaykhusraw, Cilician Armenia's suzerains. Obverse images of Georgian and Cilician Armenian rulers seated cross-legged mirror a further connection with the east. The copper coins of Giorgi III (1156–84) in Georgia and of Hetoum II and Levon III (1305–7) in Cilician Armenia all combine, in an extraordinary way, oriental, Byzantine and indigenous iconographical elements (illus. 38).

Despite these trends of oriental influence, mostly visible in the currencies struck by Georgians and

Top
**38. Copper fals of Giorgi III, king of Georgia (1156–84)**
*Diam. 22mm; wt 3.8g*
*The Barber Institute Coin Collection, GRG1; P.D. Whitting Collection*

Bottom
**39. Silver marriage tram of Hetoum I, king of Cilician Armenia (1226–70)**
The royal couple appears holding between them a long patriarchal cross. The position of Queen Zabel on the left acknowledges her seniority in terms of royal rank, and follows the protocol on Byzantine coins
*Diam. 20mm; wt 3g*
*The Barber Institute Coin Collection, AR64; P.D. Whitting Collection*

Cilician Armenians, Byzantium and Christianity remained a solid point of artistic reference. Discreet iconographical features demonstrating that connection are crosses, whether as reverse motifs or as part of Georgian and Armenian kings' regalia. More pronounced iconographical similarities are to be found on coins of King Hetoum I of Cilician Armenia (1226–70), which are modelled on Byzantine prototypes (illus. 39), and on Georgian silver imitations of Palaiologan and Trebizond coins between the 13th and 15th centuries (illus. 40).

As to the coinage of Trebizond, its iconography and inscriptions convey the continuation of Byzantine imperial ideology on the shores of the Black Sea. However, unlike their Byzantine counterparts, the emperors of Trebizond did not claim any title on their silver aspra. The imperial office of the emperors of Trebizond is only indicated by the orb cruciger they are holding, and the hand of God that crowns them. It is perhaps ironic that the dynasty of the Megaloi Komneni, stripped of their imperial title on their coins, insisted on holding the most revered symbol of universal rulership, which after 1261 is almost absent from Byzantine numismatic iconography.

# ALONG THE ROUTES OF TRADE AND WAR

The importance of the eastern Mediterranean, a traditional crossroads of people and cultures, increased from the 4th century following the move of the Roman empire's capital from Rome to Constantinople, and the subsequent shift of political and economic power to the east. Constantinople, strategically located on the Bosphorus, functioned as a major communication hub for land and sea routes. The Via Egnatia and Via Regia ensured the connection of the Byzantine capital to Dyrrachium (now Durres) on the Adriatic and to Vienna, respectively. A road leading from Chalcedon (now Kadiköy) to Nicomedia (now Izmit) assured communications with the east, while the Sea of Marmara linked the Black Sea to the Aegean. Sea transport has always been cheaper than by land and between the 4th and 7th centuries merchants made extensive use of sea routes leading from Asia Minor, the Balkans and northern Africa to Italy, Gaul, Spain and Britain. The new political geography shaped profoundly the economic role of ports: some emerged as outlets of local production and relay stations, while others declined.

**Long-distance trade** was conducted under strict state control. In the 4th century custom offices were set up in the frontier zone and the flow of foreign trade was supervised by the *comites commerciorum*, imperial officials at frontier market towns (*kommerkia*), who collected trade duties on all imports. They alone were authorized to buy silk from foreign merchants. They also ensured that foreign merchants were kept under control while staying on Byzantine soil and imposed restrictions on the export of certain commodities, such as gold and iron. The regulations were stringent and merchants who broke the law received severe fines, such as confiscation of the non-declared goods. Although regulations became more relaxed in the later Byzantine period, their very existence reflects a scrupulous effort by Byzantine authorities to control incoming and outgoing trade. In the 6th century the name of *comes commerciorum* itself changed to that of *kommerkiarios*, the Greek equivalent of the Latin term. But was the change in name only or also in the jurisdiction exercised by those imperial officials? The early sources are scarce and unenlightening. It seems that their duties were roughly the same as before, but gradually they came to focus on the silk trade, acting on behalf of the state as well as for their own profit.

The signature and sign of a *kommerkiarios'* authority was the seal created by his *boulloterion*, an iron pliers-shaped implement of variable dimensions. A lead seal provided the security of a modern registered delivery service, as the seal secured both ends of the strings attached to the sack of merchandise, making it practically impossible for a potential fraudster to open the sack without

Along the routes of trade and war

destroying the seal. Large numbers of seals have survived, compared to only a handful of *boulloteria*, and their inscriptions and iconography form a very interesting aspect of the prosopography of Byzantine society. The limited numbers of seal-finds with secure provenance, however, offer us only a glimpse into an impressive system of interregional trade and its extensive route-map, with Constantinople as a major centre of production and consumption, and final destination for many luxury items, which were transported from the four corners of the known world.

The most stable and widely accepted currency in the early medieval Mediterranean and far beyond was the Byzantine gold solidus, appropriately described by modern historians as 'the dollar of the middle ages'. Merchants, pilgrims, imperial envoys and officials carried valuable coins to faraway markets and societies, circulating Byzantine solidi as far west as Britain, and as far east as China (illus. 41). After the emergence of Islam, Muslim rulers were able to exploit the gold mines in Sudan, from where the valuable metal was carried as gold dust to city-mints in northern Africa and Egypt. By the end of the 10th century the influx of great numbers of Islamic gold dinars into neighbouring territories prompted Christian rulers in Spain, Italy and Sicily to strike dinar imitations. Islamic silver dirhams, modelled on Sasanian drachms, were also important in the trade between Muslim rulers and Europe, and significant numbers have been found in Russia, Scandinavia and northern Europe. The Byzantine response to the dirham was the silver miliaresion, similar in form, metallic value and weight to its Islamic counterpart,

but with Christian designs and the profession of Christian faith replacing the *shahada*. First introduced by Leo III (717–41), miliaresia were widely circulated across the eastern Mediterranean, the Balkans and Russia, where they prompted the emergence of similar-looking coins. After Charlemagne's coronation in 800 and the eventual Byzantine recognition of his title in 812, miliaresia had to fulfil both a political and an economic role: reverse inscriptions highlighted the status of the Byzantine ruler as the only rightful emperor of the Romans.

In 992 Byzantium's offer of trade concessions to Venice opened a new chapter in the economic relations between Byzantium and western Europe, and in the movement of people and money in the eastern Mediterranean and the Black Sea. The

Top
**45a. Florentine gold florin,
early 14th century**
*Diam. 19mm; wt 3.51g*
*The British Museum, Department of Coins
& Medals, 1885-4-5-20*

Middle
**45b. Florin-styled gold coin of Emperor
John V (1341–91), mint of
Constantinople, c. 1350–60**
*Diam. 17mm; wt 1.88g*
*Bibliothèque nationale de France, Cabinet
des Médailles, Paris: G. Schlumberger
Collection (G. Schlumberger 3,738)*

Bottom
**45c. Imitative gold florin of Omar Beg
(1341–8), Aydin**
*Diam. 21.5mm; wt 3.5g*
*The Fitzwilliam Museum, Cambridge,
Department of Coins & Medals 328-1997;
Philip Grierson Fund (PG 17,832)*

imperial privileges were conferred in return for Venice's loyalty and services to the empire, and were expressed in the form of a *chrysobull*. This document did not constitute a bilateral treaty between two equal parties since, according to Byzantium's political ideology, the emperor alone, as universal ruler by the grace of God, was in a position to grant privileges to lesser mortals. Attached to his *chrysobull* was a *bulla* (illus. 42), a splendid gold seal that added to the importance of the imperial gesture. By the 13th century things had certainly come a long way since the first offer of a *chrysobull* to a western maritime power: Seljuq sultans, Venetian *podestas*, the emperors of Trebizond and Nicaea, the Latin emperors of Constantinople (illus. 43) and the rulers of Epiros (illus. 44) all used gold seals in economic

Cy comence le liure de marc pol les meruailles dule la giant et d[m]
[...] Et des diuerses regions du monde

Pur sauoir la puve uerite de diuerses regions du mon
de. Si prenes ce liure cy et le faites lire. si y trouueres les
grandismes meruailles qui y sont escriptes. De la grant
armenie. et de perse. et des tartars. et dinde et de main
tes autres prouinces. si comme nre liure vous comptera p
ordres appertement. de quoy messire marc pol. sages z
nobles citoiens de uenisse racompte pour ce que il le

Opposite
**46. The departure of Nicolò and Matteo Polo from Byzantium (Constantinople)**
Illumination from the *Livre des Merveilles*, c. 1410–12 (author: Marco Polo; manuscript illuminator: maître de la Mazarine)
***Bibliothèque nationale de France, Département des manuscrits occidentaux, MSS Français 2810***

Below
**47. The first siege of Constantinople by the armies of the Fourth Crusade in 1203**
Illumination from the chronicle *De la Conquête de Constantinople* by Geoffrey of Villehardouin, 14th–15th century
***Bibliothèque nationale de France, Département des manuscrits occidentaux***

and diplomatic documents. Gold seals, in the grand tradition of the erstwhile exclusively Byzantine *bullae*, now told the different story of a quest for legitimacy by the area's many new masters.

Between the 13th and 15th centuries the area of the eastern Mediterranean experienced an unprecedented volume of commercial activities conducted by international merchants, who in defiance of political instability successfully carried out business within the area and as far east as India and China. Venetian ducats and grossi, Neapolitan gigliati and, to a lesser extent, Florentine florins (illus. 45) are the currencies most prominent among those mentioned in contemporary commercial and legal documents. Their wide circulation in the eastern Mediterranean influenced the form and style of local coinage. As we will soon see, coins loosely resembling or directly imitating western ones were struck by Turkmen, Seljuqs and Ottomans, Latin rulers in the Aegean and mainland Greece, as well as by Byzantines, Serbs, Bulgarians and Wallachians.

Economic and cultural encounters between East and West around the Black Sea are of particular interest. Following the arrival of the Mongols, whose rule opened up a vast road network controlled by them, Venetians and Genoese swiftly established trading posts in places previously part of the Russo-Byzantine trade network. The Bank of St George in Genoa set up an *Officium Chazariae* (Khazar Office) to monopolize the Black Sea trade, while the Pope created an archiepiscopal see at Caffa, in eastern Crimea, responsible for an area between Varna in Bulgaria and Saray on the Volga river. For western

**48. Copper follis of Roger of Salerno (1112–19), mint of Antioch, principality of Antioch**
Obv. The Virgin Mary orans/Rev. The inscription in Greek reads *Lord Aid Your Servant Roger*
*Diam. 18mm; wt 5.4g*
**The Barber Institute Coin Collection CR8;**
**P.D. Whitting Collection**

Europeans the Black Sea no longer represented a cultural and economic frontier, but rather a relay station on their way to northern Russia, China and India, and to such exotic cities as Peking, Tabriz, Delhi and Zeitum. Contemporary sources speak of merchants' enormous wealth in coins and silks, of the visits of the Venetian brothers Polo to Constantinople and Trebizond *en route* to China (illus. 46), the profitable slave trade at Caffa, a Catholic hospice in Peking, and of missionaries and Castilian envoys at the court of Timur or Tamerlane (1370–1405). All paint a colourful picture of the great western European adventure in the Near and Far East. Highly detailed Venetian and Catalan portolan maps guided merchants through the Black Sea's treacherous currents. Merchants spread a wide range of currencies to its shores between the 13th century and the late 15th. Numerous finds of silver aspra of Trebizond and their Georgian imitations along the eastern, southern and northern Black Sea coast reflect the political and economic influence of that formidable little empire, Byzantine in its political ideology and religion and at a crossroads of culture. Other coin finds further elucidate the economic profile of the Black Sea and the presence of the Golden Horde as the local regulator of trade. Alongside coins of Byzantine, Genoese, Venetian, Moldavian and other origins, there are great numbers of Golden Horde and Tartar-Genoese issues. The latter once again display cultural and religious encounters between East and West through iconography and inscriptions: a Mongol *tamgha* on the obverse is combined with a Genoese cross on the reverse.

The busy land and sea routes of southeastern Europe, frequented by merchants, pilgrims, royal envoys and ecclesiastical officials, saw a very different crowd in the late 11th century and throughout the 12th. In 1095 Pope Urban II made a passionate call at the Council of Clermont for help for the Christian communities in the east, purportedly oppressed by Muslims. The idea of an armed pilgrimage to the east spread swiftly across western Europe. Diverse groups of people, with agendas ranging from religious zeal to practical preoccupations, marched and plundered their way through German, Hungarian, Bulgarian and Byzantine territories, being responsible for unprecedented pogroms of Jewish populations, killing and being killed. Four main crusades took place between 1096 and 1204, the last of which resulted in the fall of Constantinople to armies of fellow Christians (illus. 47). The senseless destruction of the city, and the looting and dispersion of its religious treasures across Europe, left a permanent stain on relations between the Orthodox and Catholic churches, already in schism since 1054, and hampered later attempts for religious and political rapprochement between Byzantium and western Europe in the face of the Turkish advance.

The landscape that emerged in the late 12th-century eastern Mediterranean was that of a two-way traffic of people, commodities, works of art and money in the form of bullion and coinage. Crusader states in Anatolia and Syria, Seljuq and Ayyubid rulers and kings of Cilician Armenia, all considered trade as a

source of profit, and coastal cities flourished as outlets for cotton, metals and timber, spices, precious stones and silk. The coinage, which was produced by westerners and Muslims, echoes cultural and economic exchange amidst continuous strife for political control. Crusader imitative dirhams, dinars and copper folles with Greek inscriptions and Byzantine imagery (illus. 48) circulated alongside Seljuq imitations of florins and gigliati.

After 1204 Byzantium's new masters – Crusaders and Venetians – settled down in Thrace, Macedonia, parts of Epirus, Thessaly, Athens, the Peloponnese, and on the Aegean and Ionian islands. Money was needed and, after some initial import of western coins, local mints were set up in the new administrative centres. The coinage struck offers fascinating insights into the cultural and political profile of the masters of Latin Greece, whose connection to their western homelands is unmistakable. Deniers and obols locally struck are styled on contemporary western coins, and their obverse and reverse inscriptions spell out in Latin the status of the local ruler (i.e. king, prince, duke), the realm over which he ruled, and the mint where the particular coin was issued. Seals of western administrators (illus. 49), ecclesiastical officials (illus. 50) and ambassadors to Constantinople (illus. 51) follow a similar pattern, with western iconography and Latin inscriptions. In the case of intermarriage between members of Byzantine royalty and western lords, coinage issued by the latter convey through Byzantine imagery and Greek inscriptions messages of continuity and legitimacy (illus. 52).

**52. Gold ducat in the names of Emperor John V Palaiologos (1341–91) and Francesco I Gattilusio, Genoese lord of Mytilene (1355–84)**

Inspired by Venetian ducats, this unique example combines the Greek acclamation *Lord, guard Emperor John Palaiologos* on the obverse, with a Latin inscription on the reverse, which refers to Francesco I Gattilusio as lord of Mytilene (Lesbos). He married the emperor's sister and was offered the island after assisting John V to regain power. The obverse inscription probably recalls the acclamation by Francesco's soldiers, *Long live Emperor John Palaiologos*, during those extraordinary political events. The reverse inscription and image of the Genoese ruler next to a saint endorse his status and right to strike coins.

*Diam. 20.5mm; wt 3.52g*

*Muzeul Regional al Portilor de Fier, Turnu-Severin, Drobeta, Romania, no. 412; from the Dudasu Schelei hoard, Mehedinti County*

# TRAVELLING EMPERORS

The Byzantine empire restored by Michael VIII Palaiologos in 1261 was fragile, menaced by western powers with claims to the Latin Empire, by rivals in the Balkans and by new Turkish threats to the east. For a while some things worked to the empire's advantage: adroit diplomacy and the disunity of its enemies were assisted by large payments of gold, for example in about 1279/80, when Michael VIII sent 180,000 hyperpyra to the Aragonese to encourage their intervention against the Angevin kings of Sicily. By the mid-14th century, however, the empire had lost most of Asia Minor and the Balkans, while in the 15th it was little more than a few strips of land. Inevitably Byzantine coinage now had a restricted reach and would no longer be an influence on the wider world. The Byzantine state was still trying to restrict the private export of its precious metal, as stipulated in 1262 by Michael VIII in the Treaty of Nymphaeum with Genoa. Nevertheless, by the 14th century the empire could not attract or retain enough gold to maintain this metal in its coinage; the gold hyperpyron was increasingly debased and then ceased to be issued altogether.

Above, left
**53. Silver basilikon of Andronikos II and Michael IX (1294–1320)**
*Diam. 21mm; wt 2.1g*
*The Barber Institute Coin Collection, B6288; P.D. Whitting Collection*

Above, right
**54. Silver stravraton of Emperor John VIII Palaiologos (1425–48)**
*Diam. 25mm; wt 8.53g*
*The Barber Institute Coin Collection, B6492; P.D. Whitting Collection*

The hyperpyron survived as an accounting unit, used with a variety of silver coins. Known to westerners as the perper, it continued to be used to reckon money in the eastern Mediterranean, as a ghost of the Byzantine gold coinage, for the rest of the Middle Ages. The term *bezant* had a similar after-life. The name was used for many coins in the eastern Mediterranean, some (*saracen bezants*) derived from the Islamic dinar and others from Byzantine traditions, like the *white bezant* of Cyprus. The *bezant of Romania*, as Italian merchants knew it, was used in the Christian kingdom of Cilician Armenia as a multiple for its silver coinage in the late Middle Ages. It also survived in the west as a term used in heraldry for gold discs and to describe special offerings in gold made on royal and religious occasions, as occurred in 17th-century England.

In contrast to the early middle ages, western coinages now played a dominant role within the shrunken empire and more broadly in the eastern Mediterranean. In the 13th century, after the Fourth Crusade, most of the new states in the region instinctively imitated Byzantine coinage, specifically the familiar base-silver trachy coinage; these included newly independent Serbia, Bulgaria and the Latin Empire of Constantinople itself. However, things soon changed. Deniers tournois on the French model became the principal coinage in the Frankish states of Greece. At higher values, Venetian coinage dominated the Balkans and the Aegean, inspiring local imitations in Serbia and Bulgaria and among rulers throughout the Aegean archipelago, although here the coinage of Naples was also influential.

Venice's political and economic dominance of the region was incontrovertible. Probably the most important coin in the Balkans was the Venetian grosso, copied not only by the rulers of Serbia (who had their own silver mines) and Bulgaria, but also by the Byzantines themselves in the shape of the basilikon introduced by Andronikos II, probably in 1295, to replace the traditional silver trachy (illus. 53). This coin was the same weight and quality as the grosso, and its design was very similar, initially showing the emperor and his son and co-ruler Michael IX standing in place of the doge and St Mark; a later version depicts Andronikos III, the emperor's grandson, in place of Michael. By the 1320s the basilikon had become a less direct imitation of the grosso.

With the disappearance of the hyperpyron as a coin, Byzantium's coinage became one largely of silver, partly owing to the general dominance of silver in the eastern Mediterranean in the 14th and 15th centuries. Europe had been a major source of silver for the region since the 12th century. Although more local supplies were now available in Asia Minor and Serbia, for example, none was under Byzantine authority. The basilikon was a precursor of this shift, but it was the silver stavraton, a new coin worth half a hyperpyron, that was to be the main Byzantine currency from the 1350s. In appearance it was probably the least impressive high-denomination coin in the empire's entire history, featuring a relatively crude bust of Christ on the front and the emperor on the reverse (illus. 54).

The old Byzantine world was now a patchwork of

Byzantine, Frankish, Italian, Slavic and Turkish polities. To survive, the last emperors had to manoeuvre and bargain for allies and partners and often rely on sheer good luck. Several of them were in practice Turkish clients, gaining the throne during the dynastic struggles of the Palaiologan period with the assistance of Turkish rulers and surviving as their vassals, offering tribute and military support when requested. Caught in the uncomfortable position of surviving on the sufferance of the Turks and unable to resist their advance into Europe, Byzantine leaders looked to the western powers as an alternative source of crucial financial and military assistance. Several emperors made extensive visits to the west in this endeavour. In 1346 John V visited the king of Hungary and the papal court at Rome – even converting to western Christianity – yet he still ended his days wholly dependent on the Turks. Between 1400 and 1403 Manuel II made a wider tour of the west, visiting Venice, Paris, London and other places. He returned home with good wishes but no practical benefits. It was only the fortuitous arrival of the

Mongol leader Timur in 1402 that diverted the attention of the Ottoman Turks from capturing Constantinople and prolonged the empire's survival for another half century. John VIII also came west and negotiated a union between the western and eastern churches at the Council of Ferrara (1438); this again produced little practical help and was rejected by his own subjects.

Each of these visits provoked much attention in the west. John VIII was commemorated by several Renaissance artists, including Pisanello, whose medal of the emperor is among the earliest examples in the western tradition (illus. 55). Drawings of the emperor and members of his entourage made by Pisanello in Ferrara suggest that it was modelled from life, and it was probably engraved within the period 1438 to 1443. The medal has a portrait of the emperor with his name and titles in Greek on the front, and the reverse shows the emperor brought to a halt while hunting by the sign of a cross – maybe a reminiscence of the vision of Constantine the Great as well as a specific reference to the project to unify the eastern and western churches. The exotic

56. Majolica storage jar, from the region
of Florence, 1460–80
*H. 262mm; diam. (lip) 113mm*
*The British Museum, Department of
Prehistory & Europe, 1906-4-18-1*

costume of the emperor and his brother aroused
considerable interest. Pisanello's image of the
emperor seems to have remained alive for some time.
Engravings based on it were widely known, although
ironically the most famous identified the portrait as
'EL GRAN TURKO' (the Great Turk). One of these was
copied for a majolica storage jar made in Florence in
the later 15th century to give the image of a man in a
tall hat (illus. 56).

Pisanello himself was probably intending to make
a modern version of the 'medals of Constantine and
Heraclius', a set of which was formerly owned by Jean
de Berry. These are now known to have been made in
France at the turn of the 15th century and possibly
based on Manuel II Palaiologos, who was present in
Paris in 1400–2. In Italy these were thought to be
genuine ancient survivals: Constantine, the first
Christian emperor and founder of Constantinople,
and Heraklios, defeater of Persia and restorer of the
True Cross to Jerusalem. The regard given to these
medals, and the respect shown to the imperial
forebears of John VIII, who was himself about to
deliver a new Christian unity, demonstrate fascination
with Byzantine antiquity in Renaissance Italy.

NORWAY

Sigtuna •

SWEDEN

Novgorod •

LITHUANIANS

*North Sea*

SCOTLAND          DENMARK

RUSSIAN PRINCIPALITIES

Kiev •

ENGLAND

London •

KHANATE OF THE GOLDEN HORDE

• Halberstadt

• Cologne

• Tana

Moncastro •

Kaffa

GEORGIA

HOLY ROMAN EMPIRE

Paris •

Chembalo •

Soldaia

Gelati •

• Tours

Vienna •          • Budapest

*Black Sea*

FRANCE

HUNGARY

Ani •

Milan •     Venice

Sinope •

Samsun •     Trebizond

Ferrara •

Zara •

Mesembria •

Toulouse •     Marseilles •

SERBIA

Preslav •

TREBIZOND

Florence •

Dubrovnik •

• Ras

Turnovo •

Adrianople •

Nicaea •

BULGARIA

Constantinople •

CASTILE

• Ohrid

Mantzikert •

Toledo •     ARAGON

Thessaloniki •

MONGOL (ILKHAN) DOMINION

Mardin •

Rome •

Bari •

Athos •

Phocaea •

Tarsus •

Edessa •

• Cordoba

Naples •

EPIROS

Arta •

• Ephesos

CILICIAN

Antioch •

Monreale •

Cefalu •

Athens •

Antalya •

ARMENIA

Carthage •

Syracuse •

ACHAEA

Rhodes •

Nicosia •

Mistras •     • Monemvasia

MINOR CHRISTIAN STATES

*Mediterranean Sea*

Damascus •

• Acre

Alexandria •

Jerusalem •

BYZANTIUM AND ITS NEIGHBOURS, c.1265 AD

Byzantine possessions

0  100  200  300  400  500  600  700  800  Kilometres

0     100     200     300     400     500  Miles

# SELECT BIBLIOGRAPHY

## General

D. Abulafia: *Commerce and Conquest in the Mediterranean, 1100–1500* (Aldershot, 1993)

————, ed.: *The New Cambridge Medieval History*, V: *c.1198–c.1300* (Cambridge, 1999)

E. Aliyahu: *East–West Trade in the Medieval Mediterranean* (Aldershot, 1986)

A. Bellinger and P. Grierson, ed.: *Catalogue of the Byzantine Coins in the Dumbarton Oaks Collection and in the Whittemore Collection*, 5 vols (Washington, DC, 1968–99)

T. Bertelè: *Numismatique byzantine: Suivie de deux études inédites sur les monnaies des Paléologues*, French trans. and ed. by C. Morrisson (Wetteren, 1978)

O.R. Remie Constable: *Housing the Stranger in the Mediterranean World: Lodging, Trade, and Travel in Late Antiquity and the Middle Ages* (Cambridge, 2003)

P. Grierson: *Byzantine Coins* (London, 1982)

W. Hahn: *Moneta Imperii Byzantini*, 3 vols (Vienna, 1973–81)

M.F. Hendy: *Studies in Byzantine Coinage, c.300–1450* (Cambridge, 1983)

A.H.M. Jones: *The Later Roman Empire, 284–602: A Social and Administrative Survey*, 2 vols (Oxford, 1964)

A.E. Laiou, ed. in chief: *The Economic History of Byzantium* (Washington, DC, 2002)

J. Lefort, C. Morrisson and J.-P. Sodini, eds: *Les villages dans l'Empire byzantin, IVe–XVe siècle* (Paris, 2005)

R.S. Lopez: 'The Dollar of the Middle Ages', *Journal of Economic History*, XI (1951), 209–34

M. McCormick: *The Origins of the European Economy: Communications and Commerce AD 300–900* (Cambridge, 2001)

R. Macrides, ed.: *Travel in the Byzantine World* (London, 2002)

C. Morrisson: *Catalogue des monnaies byzantines de la Bibliothèque Nationale*, 2 vols (Paris, 1970)

————: 'La diffusion de la monnaie de Constantinople: routes commerciales ou routes politiques?', in *Constantinople and its Hinterland*, ed. C. Mango and G. Dagron (Aldershot, 1995), 77–89

P. Spufford: *Handbook of Medieval Exchange* (London, 1986)

————: *Money and its Use in Medieval Europe* (Cambridge, 1988)

————: *Power and Profit: The Merchant in Medieval Europe* (London, 2002)

A. Stahl: *Zecca: The Mint of Venice in the Middle Ages* (Baltimore and London, 2000)

L. Travaini: *Monete mercanti e matematica* (Rome, 2003)

P.D. Whitting: *Byzantine Coins* (London, 1973)

C. Wickham: *Framing the Early Middle Ages: Europe and the Mediterranean, 400–800* (Oxford, 2005)

W. Wroth: *Catalogue of the Imperial Byzantine Coins in the British Museum*, 2 vols (London, 1908)

————: *Catalogue of the Coins of the Vandals, Ostrogoths and Lombards, and of the Empires of Thessalonica, Nicaea and Trebizond in the British Museum* (London, 1911)

## Byzantium and the west

R. Abdy and G. Williams: 'A Catalogue of Hoards and Single Finds from the British Isles, c. AD 410–675', in *Coinage and History in the North Sea World, c. 500–1250: Essays in Honour of Marion Archibald*, ed. B.J. Cook and G. Williams (Leiden and Boston, 2006), 11–74

H.A. Adelson: *Light Weight Solidi and Byzantine Trade during the Sixth and Seventh Centuries*, American Numismatic Society, Numismatic Notes and Monographs, 138 (New York, 1957)

A.E. Arslan: 'Le monete di Ostrogoti, Longobardi e Vandali', *Milano*, XXI (1978), 1–91

A. Chédeville: 'Recherches sur la circulation de l'or en Europe occidentale du Xe à la fin du XIIe siècle d'après les cens dus au Saint-Siège', *Le Moyen Age*, 83 (1977), 413–43

B.J. Cook: 'The bezant in Angevin England', *Numismatic Chronicle*, 159 (1999), 255–75

P. Grierson: *Coins of Medieval Europe* (London, 1991)

P. Grierson and M. Blackburn: *Medieval European Coinage*, I: *The Early Middle Ages (5th–10th centuries)* (Cambridge, 1986)

P. Grierson and L. Travaini: *Medieval European Coinage*, XIV: *Italy*, III (*South Italy, Sicily, Sardinia*) (Cambridge, 1998)

A. Harris: *Byzantium, Britain and the West: The Archaeology of Cultural Identity, AD 400–650* (Stroud, 2003)

M.F. Hendy: 'From Public to Private: The Western Barbarian Coinages as a Mirror of the Disintegration of Late Roman State Structures', *Viator*, 19 (1988), 29–78.

J. Lafaurie and C. Morrisson: 'La pénétration des monnaies byzantines en Gaule', *Revue Numismatique*, 6th ser., XXIX (1987), 38–98

R.S. Lopez: 'Le problème des relations anglo-byzantines du septième au dixième siècle', *Byzantion*, XVIII (1946–8), 139–62

M.A. Metlich: *The Coinage of Ostrogothic Italy* (London, 2004)

G. Miles: *The Coinage of the Visigoths of Spain: Leogivild to Achila II* (New York, 1952)

C. Morrisson: 'La Sicile byzantine: une lueur dans les siècles obscurs', *Quaderni ticinesi di numismatica e antichità classiche*, XXVII (1998), 307–34

M. O'Hara: 'A Find of Byzantine Silver from the Mint of Rome for the Period AD 641–752', *Revue suisse de numismatique*, 64 (1985), 105-56

W.J. Tomasini: *The Barbaric Tremissis in Spain and Southern France: Anastasius to Leovigild* (New York, 1964)

L. Travaini: *La monetazione nell'Italia normana* (Rome, 1995)

————: 'The Normans between Byzantium and the Islamic World', *Dumbarton Oaks Papers*, 55 (2001), 180–97

G. Williams: 'The Circulation and Function of Coinage in Conversion-period England, c. 580–675', in *Coinage and History in the North Sea World, c. 500-1250: Essays in Honour of Marion Archibald*, ed. B.J. Cook and G. Williams (Leiden and Boston, 2006), 145–92

## Byzantium and northern, central and eastern Europe

S. Avdev: *Monetnata sistema v srednovekovna Bulgariia prez XIII–XIV vek* (Sofia, 2005)

A. Avenarius: *Die byzantinische Kultur und die Slawen: Zum Problem der Rezeption und Transformation (6. bis 12. Jahrhundert)* (Vienna, 2000)

K. Bendixen: *Denmark's Money* (Copenhagen, 1967)

A.V. Chernetsov: *Types on Russian Coins of the XIV and XV Centuries* (Oxford, 1983)

G. Custurea: *Circulatia monedei bizantine in Dobrogea (sec. IX–XI)* (Constanza, 2000)

K. Docev: *Moneti i parichno obrushtenie v Turnovo, XII–XIV vek* (Veliko Turnovo, 1992)

J.M. Fagerlie: *Late Roman and Byzantine Solidi Found in Sweden and Denmark* (New York, 1967)

J.V.A. Fine: *The Late Medieval Balkans: a Critical Survey from the Late Twelfth Century to the Ottoman Conquest* (Ann Arbor, 1983)

S. Franklin and J. Shepard: *The Emergence of Rus, 750–1200* (London and New York, 1998)

I. Hammarberg, B. Malmer and T. Zachrisson: *Byzantine Coins Found in Sweden* (Stockholm and London, 1989)

V. Ivanišević: *Serbian Medieval Coinage* (Belgrade, 2001)

I. Jordanov: *Moneti i monetno obrushtenie v srednovekovna Bulgariia, 1081–1261* (Sofia, 1984)

———: *Corpus na pechatite na srednovekovna Bulgariia* (Sofia, 2001)

M. Jovanović: *Serbian Medieval Coins* (Belgrade, 2001)

L. Kovács: *Münzen aus der ungarischen Landnahmezeit: Archäologische Untersuchung der arabischen, byzantinischen, westeuropäischen und römischen Münzen aus dem Karpatenbecken des 10. Jahrhunderts* (Budapest, 1989)

G. Majeska: *Russian Travellers to Constantinople in the Fourteenth and Fifteenth Centuries* (Washington, DC, 1984).

B. Malmer: 'The Byzantine Empire and the Monetary History of Scandinavia during the 10th and 11th centuries AD', *Les Pays du Nord et Byzance*, ed R. Zeitler (Uppsala, 1981)

D.M. Metcalf: *Coinage in South-eastern Europe, 820–1396* (London, 1979)

M. Metcalf: 'Viking-Age Numismatics, 1: Late Roman and Byzantine Gold in the Northern Lands', *Numismatic Chronicle*, 155 (1995), 413–41

T.S. Noonan: 'The Circulation of Byzantine Coins in Kievan Rus', *Byzantine Studies/Etudes byzantines*, VII/2 (1980), 143–81

E. Oberländer-Târnoveanu: 'From Perperi Auri ad Sagium Vicine to Perperi: Money of Account of Byzantine-Balkan Origin in Wallachia (Thirteenth to Nineteenth Centuries)', *130 Years since the Establishment of the Modern Romanian Monetary System* (Bucharest, 1997), 97–182

———: 'Notes on the Beginnings of the Bulgarian Medieval Coinage', *The Bulgarian Lands in the Middle Ages, 7th–18th Centuries: International Conference. A Tribute to the 70th Anniversary of Prof. Alexander Kuzev, Varna, September 12th–14th, 2002, Acta Musei Varnaensis*, III/1 (2003), 183–214

D. Obolensky: *The Byzantine Commonwealth: Eastern Europe, 500–1453* (New York, 1971)

V. Penna: 'Το Βυζάντιο και οι λαοί της κεντρικής και ανατολικής Ευρώπης, η νομισματική μαρτυρία (8ος–11ος αι. μ.Χ.)', *Ιστορικογεωγραφικά* 3 (1989–90), 53–97

E.J. Prawdzic-Golemberski and D.M. Metcalf: 'The Circulation of Byzantine Coins on the South-eastern Frontiers of the Empire', *Numismatic Chronicle*, 73 (1963), 83–92

A. Radushev and G. Zhekov: *Katalog na bulgarskite srednovekovni moneti, IX–XV vek*, (Sofia, 1999)

S.W. Reinert: 'What the Genoese cast upon Helena Dragash's Head: Coins not Confecti', *Byzantinsche Forschungen* XX (1994), 235–46

L. Réthy and G. Probszt: *Corpus Nummorum Hungariae* (Graz, 1958)

M.P. Sotnikova and I.G. Spasski: *Russian Coins of the X–XI Centuries AD* (Oxford, 1982)

J. Steen Jensen: *Tusindtallets Danske Mønter fra Den kongelige Mønt- og Medaillesamling* (Copenhagen, 1995)

P. Stephenson: *Byzantium's Balkan Frontiers: A Political Study of the Northern Balkans* (Cambridge, 2000)

E.S. Stoljarik: *Essays on Monetary Circulation in the North-western Black Sea Region in Late Roman and Byzantine Periods, late 3rd Century – early 13th Century AD* (Odessa, 1992)

E. Theoklieva-Stoytcheva, *Medieval Coins from Mesembria* (Sofia, 2001)

Y. Youroukova, 'La circulation des monnaies byzantines en Bulgarie VIe – Xe s.', *I Miedzynarodowy Kongres Archeologii Slowianskiej, Warszawa 14–18 IX 1965*, VI (Warsaw, 1968), 128–43

## Byzantium's eastern neighbours

F. Babinger: *Mehmed the Conqueror and his Time* (Princeton, 1978)

M. Bates: 'Byzantine Coinage and its Imitations, Arab Coinage and its Imitations: Arab-Byzantine Coinage', *Aram*, 6 (1994), 381–403

P.Z. Bedoukian: *Coinage of Cilician Armenia* (Danbury, CT, 1979)

M. Broom: *A Handbook of Islamic Coins* (London 1985)

C. Foss: 'Syria in Transition, AD 550–750: An Archaeological Approach', *Dumbarton Oaks Papers*, 51 (1997), 189–269

E.S. Georganteli: 'Monetary Transaction and Cultural Exchange in Medieval Anatolia', in *Eat, Drink and be Merry: Papers from the Thirty-fifth Spring Symposium of Byzantine Studies in Honour of A. Bryer*, ed. L. Brubaker and K. Linardou (London, 2006)

N. Lowick: *Coinage and History of the Islamic World*, Variorum Reprints, ed. J. Cribb (London, 1990)

N. Lowick, S. Bendall and P. Whitting: *The Mardin Hoard: Islamic Countermarks on Byzantine Folles* (London, 1977)

C. Morrisson: 'Le monnayage omeyyade et l'histoire administrative et économique de la Syrie', in *La Syrie de Byzance à l'Islam, VIIe-VIIIe siècles: Actes du Colloque international, Lyon-Maison de l'Orient Méditerranéen, Paris, Institut du Monde Arabe, 1990*, ed. P. Canivet and J. Rey-Coquais (Institut Français de Damas, Damascus, 1992), 309–21

V. Nersessian: *Treasures from the Ark: 1700 Years of Armenian Christian Art* (London, 2001)

E.A. Pachomov, *Coins of Georgia* (Tbilisi, 1970) [in Georgian]

W.F. Spengler and W.G. Sayles, *Turkoman Figural Bronze Coins and their Iconography*, 2 vols (Lodi, WI, 1992–6)

R. Shukurov: 'Turkoman and Byzantine Self-identity: Some Reflections on the Logic of the Title Making in Twelfth- and Thirteenth-century Anatolia', in *Eastern Approaches to Byzantium: Papers from the Thirty-third Spring Symposium of Byzantine Studies, University of Warwick, Coventry, March 1999*, ed. A. Eastmond (Aldershot, 2001), 259–76

M. Tsotselia, *History and Coin Finds in Georgia: Sasanian and Byzantine Coins from Tsitelitskaro* (AD 641) (Wetteren, 2002)

I. Tsukhishvili and G. Depeyrot: *History and Coin Finds in Georgia: Late Roman and Byzantine Hoards (4th–13th c.)* (Wetteren, 2003)

J. Walker: *A Catalogue of the Arab-Byzantine and Post-Reform Umaiyad Coins* (London, 1956)

N. Zekos: 'The Tomb of the Empress Maria Botaneiate on Mt. Papikion', *Caucasica, The Journal of Caucasian Studies*, vol. 1 (1998), 199–212

### Routes of trade and war

H. Antoniadis-Bibicou: *Recherches sur les douanes à Byzance: L'octava, le kommerkion et les commerciaires* (Paris, 1963)

J. Baker: 'Coin Circulation in Early Fourteenth-century Thessaly and South-Eastern Mainland Greece', in *Χρήμα και Αγορά στην Εποχή των Παλαιολόγων*, ed. N.G. Moschonas (Athens, 2003), 293–336

M. Balard: *La Romanie génoise (XIIIe–début du XVe siècle)*, Ecole française de Rome (Rome, 1978)

———: *La mer Noire et la Romanie génoise (XIIIe-XVe siècles)*, Variorum Reprints (London, 1989)

A. Blanchet: 'Les dernières monnaies d'or des empereurs de Byzance', *Revue Numismatique* (1910), 78–90

A.A. Bryer: *The Empire of Trebizond and the Pontos*, Variorum Reprints (London, 1980)

J. Chrysostomides: 'Venetian Commercial Privileges under the Palaeologi', *Studi Veneziani*, XII (1970), 267–356

W.R. Day, Jr: 'Early Imitations of the Gold Florin of Florence and the Imitation Florin of Chivasso in the Name of Theodore I Paleologus, Marquis of Montferrat (1306–1338)', *Numismatic Chronicle*, 164 (2004), 183–200

A. Dunn: 'The Kommerkiarios, the Apotheke, the Dromos, the Vardarios and the West', *Byzantine and Modern Greek Studies*, XVII (1993), 3–24

K. Fleet, *European and Islamic Trade in the Early Ottoman State* (Cambridge, 1999)

P. Grierson: 'La moneta veneziana nell'economia mediterranea del trecento e quattrocento', *La civiltà veneziana del Quattrocento* (Venice 1957)

———: 'Commerce in the Dark Ages: A Critique of the Evidence', *Transactions of the Royal Historical Society*, 5th ser., IX (1959), 123–40

———: 'Byzantine Gold Bullae, with a Catalogue of those at Dumbarton Oaks', *Dumbarton Oaks Papers*, 20 (1966), 239–44

D. Jacoby: 'Changing Economic Patterns in Latin Romania: The Impact of the West', in *The Crusades from the Perspective of Byzantium and the Muslim World*, ed. A.E. Laiou and R.P. Mottahedeh (Washington, DC, 2001), 198–235

C. King: *The Black Sea: A History* (Oxford, 2004)

M. Koromila: *The Greeks and the Black Sea* (Athens, 2002)

A.E. Laiou: 'The Byzantine Economy in the Mediterranean Trade System: Thirteenth–Fifteenth Centuries', *Dumbarton Oaks Papers*, 34/35 (1980–81), 177–222

———: 'Byzantine Trade with Christians and Muslims and the Crusades', with an appendix by C. Morrisson, in *The Crusades from the Perspective of Byzantium and the Muslim World*, ed. A.E. Laiou and R.P. Mottahedeh (Washington, DC, 2001), 157–96

R.-J. Lilie: *Handel und Politik: zwischen dem byzantinischen Reich und den italienischen* (Amsterdam, 1984)

D.M. Metcalf: *Coinage of the Crusades and the Latin East in the Ashmolean Museum, Oxford* (London, 1995)

C. Morrisson: 'Coin Usage and Exchange Rates in Badoer's *Libro dei Conti*', *Dumbarton Oaks Papers*, 54 (2001), 217–44

E. Oberländer-Târnoveanu: '"Immo verius sub ducati Venetiarum communis proprio stigmate". La question des émissions d'or de Francesco Ier Gattilusio, seigneur de Metelino (1355–1384)', *Revue Numismatique*, 160 (2004), 223–40

N. Oikonomides: 'Silk Trade and Production in Byzantium from the Sixth to the Ninth Century: The Seals of kommerkiarioi', *Dumbarton Oaks Papers*, 40 (1986), 33–53

J. Porteous: 'Crusader Coinage with Greek or Latin Inscriptions', in K.M. Setton (general editor), *A History of the Crusades*, VI (Madison, WI, 1989), 354–420

F. Thierry and C. Morrisson: 'Sur les monnaies byzantines trouvées en Chine', *Revue Numismatique*, XXXVI (1994), 109–45

F. Thiriet: *La Romanie vénitienne au moyen-âge* (Paris, 1959)

A. Walmsley: 'Production, Exchange and Regional Trade in the Islamic East Mediterranean: Old Structures, New Systems?', in *The Long Eighth Century*, ed. I.L. Hansen and C. Wickham (Leiden, 2000), 265–343

E.A. Zachariadou: *Trade and Crusade: Venetian Crete and the Emirates of Menteshe and Aydin (1300–1415)* (Venice, 1983)

### Travelling emperors

H.C. Evans, ed.: *Byzantium: Faith and Power (1261–1557)* (New York, 2004), 527–36

S.K. Scher, ed.: *The Currency of Fame: Portrait Medals of the Renaissance* (New York, 1994)

L. Syson and D. Gordon: *Pisanello: Painter to the Renaissance Court* (London, 2001)

R. Weiss: 'The Medieval Medallions of Constantine and Heraclius', *Numismatic Chronicle*, 3 (1963), 129–44

———: *Pisanello's Medallion of the Emperor John VIII Palaeologus* (London, 1966)